P9-CCW-880

Other PaperStars by Jean Fritz

TRAITOR

THE CASE OF
BENEDICT ARNOLD

· *Jean Fritz* ·

The Putnam & Grosset Group

Grateful acknowledgment is given to the following sources for
permission to reproduce the illustrations in this book:
Yale University Art Gallery
(page 105)
Emmet Collection
Print Collection
Art, Prints and Photographs Division
The New York Public Library
Astor, Lenox and Tilden Foundations
(page 139)
Yale University Art Gallery
Gift of Ebenezer Baldwin. B. A., in 1808
(page 163)
Maps drawn by Carolyn Craven

A PaperStar Book,
published in 1997 by The Putnam & Grosset Group,
200 Madison Avenue, New York, NY 10016. PaperStar Books
and the PaperStar logo are trademarks of
The Putnam Berkley Group, Inc. Originally published in 1981 by
G. P. Putnam's Sons. Published simultaneously in Canada.
Printed in the United States of America.
Book design by Kathleen Westray
Library of Congress Cataloging-in-Publication Data
Fritz Jean.   Traitor, the case of Benedict Arnold.
Bibliography: p.   Includes index.
Summary: A study of the life and character
of the brilliant Revolutionary War general who
deserted to the British for money.
1. Arnold, Benedict, 1741–1801—Juvenile literature.
2. American loyalists—Biography Juvenile literature.
3. Generals—United States—Biography—Juvenile literature.
4. United States, Continental Army—Biography—Juvenile literature.
[1. Arnold, Benedict, 1741–1801.   2. American loyalists.
3. Generals.   4. United States—History—Revolution,
1775–1783—Biography]   I. Title.
E278.A7F73   973.3'82'0924   [B]   [92]   81-10584
ISBN 0-698-11553-8
30

*To Cheryl Matthews
and with thanks to Bette Diver
and the staff of the Dobbs Ferry library*

chapter · 1 ·

WHEN BENEDICT ARNOLD WAS A teenager, some people in his hometown of Norwich, Connecticut, predicted that he'd grow up to be a success. Others said, No. Benedict Arnold would turn out badly. As it happened, everyone was right. Benedict Arnold succeeded beyond anyone's wildest expectations "the bravest of the brave," George Washington called him in 1777. Yet three years later he was described as "the veriest villain villain of centuries past," and no one would have argued with that.

The trouble was not that Benedict Arnold changed, but that since his teenage years, he changed so little. Born on January 14, 1741, Benedict started life as one of the lucky ones, the only son in a prosperous family. When the Arnolds went to church, they walked down the aisle to the front pews reserved for the "first families" of Norwich. When it was time for Benedict to study seriously, he was sent away to a private school in

Canterbury, Connecticut, where he learned Latin and mathematics. While he was away, his mother kept him supplied with chocolates and long, gloomy letters, begging him to be good. At school he was known for his hot temper and for his loud voice, which his teachers tried but failed to correct. Furthermore, as he admitted later, he was a coward.

Still, when life was easy, being a coward was probably no serious handicap. But Benedict Arnold's life was never easy for long. His fortunes raged up and down as if he were the center of a private storm system. The first storm hit in 1755 when Benedict was fourteen; he was suddenly withdrawn from school because there was no money to pay for it. If his father could have borrowed money, he probably would have, but there was no one who would lend him money now. Mr. Arnold, at one time a successful merchant, was one of those men unable or unwilling to live within his income. For years he had been borrowing, borrowing, borrowing—investing in one scheme after another, confident each time that this scheme was the one that would make him really rich. But nothing worked out and now his creditors were not only demanding their money back, they were accusing him of cheating. A failure and a disgrace, Mr. Arnold gradually gave up on life and drank to forget his despair.

People, of course, felt sorry for poor Mrs. Arnold, such a pious woman from such a fine old Connecticut family. Only recently she had lost two of her three daughters during an epidemic of yellow fever and here she was now with a husband who had ruined both his business and his reputation. Although her neighbors brought gifts of food and clothing to help out from time to time, they whispered and pecked at the scandal behind her back. Of course Mrs. Arnold knew about the whispering, so it could not have been easy for her to walk down to the front row of the Norwich church on a Sunday morning. But she did. Every Sunday. It could not have been easy for Benedict either. Nor for his older sister Hannah.

But Benedict had more to contend with than whispers behind his back. Perhaps because he was a coward, perhaps because he was short as a young man, perhaps because he was so obviously embarrassed when he was seen leading his drunken father home from a tavern, Benedict became the butt of other boys' jokes. One way or another, he put up with it for a while. But sometime during that year, Benedict determined that he would not be a loser any longer. He would be a winner. He would not stand for criticisms or slurs on either his honor or his family's honor. Indeed, he would force people to look up to him. And he would do all this by learning to be brave.

Fortunately, Benedict Arnold, though short, had a strong, nimble body. When he decided to fight his tormentors, he generally picked on boys who were bigger than he was and he generally won. As he became more confident, he became more able and more daring. He leaped over wagons in the road; he climbed the masts of ships in the harbor and performed tricks. Then he would challenge anyone to do better. He was such a natural athlete, it didn't take long for him to prove his bravery, not only to himself but to the boys in town. To his surprise, they began seeking him out, following him to see what adventures he would think up next, cheering him on. This was a new and heady experience for Benedict Arnold. It was as if up to now he'd been drifting along under a feeble breeze but suddenly his sails had filled and a fresh wind was sweeping him full-tilt ahead and he was glory-bound. Oh, there was nowhere he couldn't go now! Nothing he couldn't do! Bravery: it was the answer to everything. It was all that mattered. Perhaps it was during this period that he carved his initials in the woodwork of the Norwich house. On windowsills. High up on beams. In room after room. B.A. B.A. B.A. It was as if he had to make his mark every minute and every place. "Watch me," he seemed to say. "I'll show you."

And indeed he did show Norwich. One day in front of a crowd of boys he climbed the dam of a millpond, grabbed a slippery arm of the mill wheel, and hanging on with all his might, he went the full circle with the turning wheel. Into the water out of sight. Up again, dripping, laughing—high into the air. Then he jumped free, splashed into the pond and swam ashore. This caused such a sensation that he was often asked to repeat the performance. And he often did.

Once when the whole town had gathered to watch a house burn down after the firefighters had given up on it, Benedict Arnold suddenly appeared on the housetop. With flames rising on both sides, he walked the full length of the ridgepole that ran down the peak of the roof, his arms outstretched to help him keep his balance. The people held their breath—a crazy, fool thing to do, they said, but Benedict Arnold came through unharmed.

Once with the help of a friend he turned a cannon over on the village green, filled it with gunpowder and thrust a lighted torch into the muzzle. Although the cannon backfired and singed Benedict's hair and face, it exploded with such a glorious bang, it was worth it. Indeed, in one way Benedict was attracting as much attention in town as his father was in another, and although poor Mrs. Arnold scolded and worried and prayed, it did no good. Benedict thrived on being noticed and never missed a chance to prove what a daredevil he was.

On Thanksgiving Eve when the townspeople customarily lit bonfires on the surrounding hills, Benedict decided to build a bonfire such as Norwich had never seen before. To the top of the highest hill Benedict and his friends dragged enough lumber and kindling to guarantee a spectacular blaze. Then from the local shipyard Benedict stole tar barrels to add to the flames. He was rolling a barrel up the hill when a constable stopped him. Since Benedict Arnold had made it a habit to do just one thing when he was crossed, he did it now. He took off his coat, rolled up his sleeves, and challenged the constable to fight. Described as a "stout, grave man," the constable simply took Benedict by the collar and marched him home to his mother.

Poor Mrs. Arnold. It was obvious that in spite of

prayers and entreaties, she couldn't handle Benedict. So she arranged for him to be apprenticed to her cousins, the two Lathrop brothers who ran a large apothecary store in town. He would live with them, working and learning the trade until he was twenty-one. Then he would be on his own, free to go into business for himself or do whatever he wanted.

Benedict undoubtedly felt confined, shut inside a store with boxes and bottles of herbs, powder, spices and elixirs of all kinds which he had to learn to mix into medicines and ointments. Sometimes he waited on customers, handing a plug of tobacco across the counter, reaching into a bottle of live leeches. Sometimes he might even apply a leech to the skin of a person who thought he'd feel better if he were bled. Sometimes he engaged in actual business transactions, helping to order and buy stock for the store. Like many apothecary stores, the Lathrop establishment dealt in a variety of goods besides medicines—wines, for instance, imported silks and other luxury items. And the Lathrops were successful. They lived in a richly furnished mansion with formal gardens behind it; they had slaves to wait on them and a fancy chaise to ride in.

However Benedict might chafe at the humdrum aspects of his work, he would have enjoyed living in such high style and helping to make so much money. Like his father, he loved money. He liked to show off his possessions, to sport elegant clothes, to walk around in dapper shoes. Benedict had a special craving for shoes. He dreamed of the day when he might have a whole wardrobe of them, stylish pointy-toed shoes—some with square, some with oval, buckles, a few perhaps with sparkles inlaid in the buckles. He'd have dress-up shoes with red heels, everyday shoes with black heels, and boots of every kind. Of course Benedict wanted an active life, but if he couldn't have that, he'd settle for a rich, showy one. But what he really wanted was both.

Indeed he missed the danger he'd pursued in his more carefree days. If he could only have gone to war! But as an apprentice and underage as well, he had no chance to join the only war that was going on. The English were fighting the French for control of North America and there was nothing Benedict Arnold would have relished more than a chance to beat up some Frenchmen. Like most New England Protestants, he hated the French, not only because they were England's traditional enemy but because they were Catholics and wanted (so people said) to force their "popish" ways upon the New World.

In any case, the war was too far away to have much to do with him until suddenly in the summer of 1757 it moved practically next door. The French with their Indian allies came right into the province of New York and threatened Fort William Henry, the British garrison at the southern tip of Lake George, less than one hundred miles from the Massachusetts border. Who could feel safe now? In a panic New Englanders called for all available men to join the local militia and march on the double to Lake George. The Lathrops agreed that although Benedict was only sixteen, he was available.

So Benedict went off, his musket over his shoulder, his hopes high. Among those streaming north was another young Connecticut man, a born fighter like Benedict Arnold and wild for battle. Ethan Allen was nineteen years old and though he and Benedict didn't meet on this expedition, they would later, whether they liked it or not. At the moment, however, they were both doomed to disappointment. While still on the road, they heard that the fighting was over and with less than two weeks of service, both young men were sent home. Not only had they missed out on the action, but the French and Indians had won. So all Benedict's army experience did for him was to give him a little exercise and fan his hatred for the French.

As it turned out, New England was not invaded and Benedict had to settle down to his old routine. Part of him, however, hungered, as it always would, for action. Perhaps not even Benedict realized how deep this hunger went until the day that the big storm hit Norwich. No one in town had ever seen such a storm. It was so horrendous, it seemed supernatural—as if God Himself were on the warpath. In those days many people believed that God sent earthquakes, hurricanes and other natural disasters to punish mankind for its sins. So all over Norwich people were falling on their knees, praying for deliverance. But not Benedict Arnold. There was something about the fury and violence of the storm that excited him. He leaped up on the counter and with each flash of lightning, with each clap of thunder, he cheered the storm on. It was as if the sky had gathered all its forces together in one place and Benedict, laughing, shaking his fists in the air, dared the storm to do its worst. Those who saw him and those who heard about his counter-top demonstration said that Benedict Arnold was foolhardy and blasphemous. He would certainly turn out badly.

Benedict himself had few thoughts about being good or bad. He simply knew what he wanted and was eager to go after it. But he would have to wait until he was twenty-one.

chapter

· 2 ·

THE YEAR 1760 TURNED OUT TO be a landmark for the American colonies although no one knew it at the time. In the first place, the war ended that year when the British army beat the French and took possession of Canada. In the second place, Great Britain had a new king— twenty-two-year-old George III, who was tall, imposing and full of fatherly-sounding words about his subjects. The first reports about him were complimentary and bursting with optimism about the future. Soon, however, another note crept into the news from across the sea. There were upsetting rumors: this king had different ideas about governing the colonies. He believed that they should help pay for the expensive war that had just ended; he believed in strict obedience and even proposed (contrary to all past policy) that England could and should impose taxes on the colonies.

So far, however, this was all talk and although

Americans grumbled and worried, they went about their business as usual. As for Benedict, he was too busy with his private life to bother about George III. Benedict's mother had died the year before and the Norwich house was being run now by his sister Hannah, a year older than he was. Since his mother's death, his father was drinking more heavily than ever. In May he was arrested for public drunkenness, for behaving without "Understanding and Reason" and violating the laws of the colony. Young Benedict would have come to the rescue as he must have time and again in the past. But this period in Benedict's life was almost over. His father died in 1761. The following year Benedict turned twenty-one and was at last free to do as he pleased. And he knew exactly what he wanted to do.

Benedict Arnold planned to open his own apothecary store and become rich like the Lathrops. He would go to New Haven, a town of 5,000 which had no such store yet, and he would dazzle the people with his stock of imported goods. With 500 pounds that the Lathrops gave him on completion of his service, Benedict went to London to select his merchandise. And what a figure he cut! Short as he was, he was a thickset, well-built man with a certain nobility of bearing. His eyes, an intense blue verging on violet, demanded attention and his large chin was thrust forward as if it meant to follow through on that demand. Dressed in a style that he thought appropriate to his new station and dizzy with a sense of his own importance, Benedict whirled through London on a grand buying spree.

Maps, pictures, paints, watches, wines he ordered for the store. Dress goods, teas, sugar, books. A chariot for himself. Clothes and more clothes. What he couldn't pay for, he bought on credit. A man of large ideas, he refused to be tied down to petty details of accounting. It would all sort itself out in the end, he figured. At the moment all he had to do was to sign his name, so he signed and signed. Then he went back to New Haven.

When he opened his store on the New Haven waterfront, he advertised himself as "B. Arnold, Druggist, Bookseller, etc. from London." People watching him ride around in his chariot must have thought he was already a success. They knew that he had ten horses in his stable and they noted that he dressed in the latest fashion, right down to his pointy-toed shoes. Even the Latin motto he chose for himself had an impressive ring: "*Sibi Totique.*" Translated, it meant "For self and all." And as the motto suggested, Benedict intended to take care of himself first.

As time went on, however, his creditors realized that the "all" in his motto did not include them. When they billed him for the money he owed, he waved them off. Later, he said. Later. When they threatened to take him to court, Benedict acted as if he'd been insulted. As if his honor had been questioned. As if his signature alone were not enough. Finally, in 1763, his creditors carried out their threats and had him thrown in jail for his debts. He stayed there for six weeks. Then the court allowed him to settle with his creditors by paying a few shillings on every pound he owed. It was an easy way out for Benedict. He sold part of his stock, scraped up the required number of shillings and was back in business again. Unrepentant. Proud as ever. Ready to take on new risks.

No matter how often Benedict Arnold met up with financial setbacks, he was never moved to modify his style of living. On the contrary. Instead of spending less and trying to live within his income, invariably he rushed headlong into a project that involved spending more money. So now he decided that running an apothecary store was neither profitable nor exciting enough. He would have a second career. He would invest in ships and sail to distant ports. He would become a trader. Instead of being "Dr. Arnold" (which is what a trained apothecary was called), he would be "Captain Arnold"—in command of vessels, courting danger, buying and selling on a grand scale. First he would need money but he had the answer to that. He would sell the family home in Norwich, bring Hannah to New Haven, and let her run the store while he was away on his trading expeditions.

Fortunately Hannah was agreeable. She adored her brother and though she had recently thought of marriage, she had given up that idea and was ready to do whatever Benedict asked. Indeed, it was because of Benedict that she'd lost out on what may have been her only romance. She knew, of course, that Benedict wouldn't approve of her suitor so she hadn't told him, but one day when he came from New Haven on an unexpected visit, Benedict found the man there. He was obviously courting Hannah. And he was a *Frenchman*! Furious that a Frenchman would have the impudence to court his sister, Benedict sent him out of the house and warned him not to come back. Yet Hannah and the Frenchman must have been in love, for he did come back and on one of his visits he was again surprised by Benedict. This time Benedict stood outside and when the Frenchman came out the door, Benedict fired his pistol into the air. The next time, Benedict said, he would shoot to kill. But there was never a next time. The Frenchman left town and for the rest of her life Hannah behaved as a dutiful sister.

For the next ten years Benedict spent a major part of his time at sea, sailing south to the Caribbean islands, his boat loaded with horses and lumber to be traded for rum, sugar, molasses and whatever European goods could be picked up here and there. Then back home to exchange this cargo for woolen goods and cheese to take to Canada, where he would load up on horses for the next trip south. Benedict learned all the tricks of his trade, how to cut corners, how to avoid revenue laws, how to drive fast bargains. He made money, but nevertheless he continued to accumulate debts and creditors who automatically became "blockheads" in Benedict's language if they had the "impertinence" to insist on prompt payment.

Nor was it only creditors with whom he had trouble. All his life he picked up enemies wherever he went. And no wonder. Benedict Arnold stood an around-the-clock watch to see that no one discredited his honor. Most men in the eighteenth

century were touchy about their honor—the very
core, it seemed, of their masculinity, but Benedict
was even more sensitive than most. No one had
better cross him. Or slight him. Or speak
disrespectfully to him. He had learned as a boy in
Norwich what to do with people like this. Even
now he wasn't above putting up his fists or
deliberately kicking an offender in the shins, but
more often these days he challenged the man to a
duel. He fought a James Brookman in the West
Indies. He ran across Hannah's Frenchman in the
Honduras and wounded him in a duel. He took
exception to a British sea captain's accusing him of
having no manners. On this occasion Benedict had
forgotten the captain's dinner invitation the
previous evening and was on the point of
explaining, but after this insult, Benedict would not
stoop to explain. Only a duel would settle the
matter. So seconds were chosen, a time and place
agreed upon, and the contenders met. At the last
minute, however, the British captain decided that
neither his honor nor Benedict's was worth dying
for, so he put away his pistol and apologized.

At sea Benedict Arnold was more like his old
carefree, adventurous self. Indisputably in charge of
his crew, out of reach of irritating letters from
creditors, under no social or business obligations,
he had only nature to contend with. And the fiercer
the weather, the stronger he felt. Indeed there were
times when Benedict was riding out a storm, that he
felt like a boy again, spinning around on a mill
wheel, walking a ridgepole on a burning roof.

Yet for all his scrappiness Benedict had not lost

his ability to rally men around him when he needed
them. In 1764 Peter Boles, one of his own
crewmen, proved this. Angry because he hadn't
been paid, Peter informed the customs officers in
New Haven that Benedict Arnold had been
smuggling West Indian goods (sugar, molasses,
rum) into town without paying a tax. Since most
merchants in New England were smuggling these
days to avoid the new Sugar Act, Benedict had no
trouble arousing a party of men to take care of Peter
Boles. Together they took him to the town
whipping post, gave him forty lashes, and then ran
him out of town. This was like the old days in
Norwich: Benedict leading his friends on a wild
spree!

But the Sugar Act was just the beginning. The
government was obviously committed now to a tax
program which everyone had feared. In 1765 the
Stamp Act was introduced with a tax on
newspapers, almanacs, pamphlets and all legal
documents. Although this proved unenforceable
and lasted only a year, other taxes followed but
these too were repealed until only the tea tax
remained. Still, the colonists would not accept any
tax. They quit drinking tea, raised liberty poles,
harassed the British troops who were stationed in
Boston, and in general made life miserable for
anyone sympathetic to the British policy. At each
new provocation, Benedict Arnold fumed. "Good
God!" he wrote impatiently at one point. "Are
Americans all asleep and tamely giving up their
glorious liberties?"

Yet there were occasions of relative peace between bursts of violence and it was in 1767 during one of these lulls that Benedict married. He had just turned twenty-six and his bride, Peggy Mansfield, daughter of the town's high sheriff, was twenty-two. In the next five years Peggy bore three sons (Benedict, Richard, and Henry) and was, as far as is known, a good enough wife except for one failing. She simply would not write letters to Benedict when he was away, at least not often enough to suit him. Once after not hearing from her for four months, Benedict wrote in exasperation: "I am now under the greatest Anxiety & Suspense, not knowing whether I write to the Dead or Living." After still another long silence, he signed himself, "your affectionate & Unhappy Benedict Arnold."

In 1773 Benedict left the sea and took up full-time residence in New Haven. Perhaps he could no longer endure the long, silent separations. Likely he wanted to stay in close touch with the growing conflict in the colonies. Certainly he wanted to supervise the completion of his new home. This house was to be the fulfillment of a dream—the most elaborate residence in New Haven, built on the waterfront on a two-acre lot already planted with one hundred fruit trees. Benedict had thought of everything for his house: marble fireplaces, white pillars, fluted domes, graveled walks, a fancy coach house, two wine closets, and even a secret staircase. And there would be a wardrobe especially designed for his many shoes.

But Benedict Arnold was never to live in peace in

his dream house nor was he the kind of man to choose peace, if he had the choice. The struggle over government policy was not just between the British and the colonists; for years it was within the colonies themselves—between Tories (those sympathetic to England) and Patriots, who tried in every way to keep the Tories quiet or to scare them off. In Massachusetts, for instance, one outspoken Tory was persuaded to hold his tongue after he found his horse with its mane cut off and its tail shaved clean. In New Haven Benedict Arnold and a rough crowd of radical Patriots paid midnight calls on offending Tories. After these calls the Tories generally decided that, for the sake of their health, they should leave town. In addition, there were also factions among the Patriots themselves. At the head of the conservative branch of the Patriot party, Colonel David Wooster, a veteran of the French and Indian War, often opposed Arnold's terrorist methods.

By 1774, however, it appeared that the enemy would soon be the British army itself, and all over the country Americans were preparing themselves for the worst. In December 1774, Benedict was one of sixty to join the newly formed militia company in New Haven; in March of the following year he was elected captain. He was thirty-four years old but he took command with the same gusto as if he'd been fifteen. He loved every part of the job. Giving orders. Drilling. Parading. Dressing up. Actually he took as much pride in his men's appearance as in his own. The New Haven company, in their scarlet tunics, white waistcoats and breeches and black half-leggings, surely looked as smart as any British troops who might march out of Boston.

In April the British troops did march out of Boston and after the first shots were fired in Lexington, fast-riding couriers spread the alarm throughout the country. When the news reached New Haven, Benedict Arnold immediately made ready to go north and take part in the action. While he was assembling his men, a town meeting was called to decide what New Haven should do. Should the militia company respond at all? The citizens hesitated. Maybe the affair at Lexington was just an isolated fracas, they said. Maybe nothing more would happen. Why rush off now? Wait and see, the town decided.

Wait? When Benedict Arnold heard the vote, he exploded. "Damn the town meeting!" he cried. "None but Almighty God shall prevent my marching."

But first he needed ammunition. He sent to the selectmen for the keys to the powder house. Colonel Wooster was in charge and when he refused to give them up, Benedict Arnold said he would wait just five minutes. If he didn't have the keys then, he'd break down the door.

It was only too clear that Benedict Arnold meant what he said. He made an enemy of David Wooster, but he got the keys and rode off at the head of his company—forty-eight men and a valet to take care of his clothes. At the last minute Benedict signed a statement which denied that the town had any thought of rebellion, but Benedict was just pacifying the selectmen. In his heart he knew that war lay ahead. What was more, he was glad of it. All he hoped was that as an early comer he'd be assigned an important role.

On the way north the New Haven men met others—militia companies like their own, farm boys traveling singly or in twos and threes, all bound for Cambridge, the headquarters of American resistance. A few were traveling the opposite way, returning from Cambridge on various missions; all these carried the same reports. There was not enough ammunition in Cambridge, not enough firearms, scarcely any heavy artillery. How could they fight? How could they supply themselves quickly enough for the next battle if there was one? Colonel Samuel Parsons, an old friend of Benedict Arnold's who had just left Cambridge, was extremely troubled about the arms shortage. As the two men stopped on the road to talk, Benedict happened to mention Fort Ticonderoga on Lake Champlain. Perhaps he had visited it on one of his Canadian trading expeditions; in any case, he claimed that in this nearby British fort there were some eighty cannons, twenty brass guns, as well as a large supply of smaller arms and ammunition. Moreover, he said, the fort was not heavily guarded.

Both men agreed that the supplies at Fort Ticonderoga would certainly come in handy. Besides, if Americans had possession of the fort, they would have a distinct advantage in any war that might lie ahead. When they had finished talking, the two men went their separate ways. Apparently, however, as they rode along, they continued to think about Fort Ticonderoga. When Samuel Parsons reached Hartford, he talked to friends who agreed to borrow money from the treasury, raise their own troops, and try to capture Fort Ticonderoga. When Benedict Arnold reached Massachusetts, he went straight to the Committee of Safety, in charge of military matters. Benedict not only offered to lead an expedition against Fort Ticonderoga, he assured the committee he'd deliver the fort in short order. Indeed, wasn't this just the chance he'd been waiting for?

Captain Arnold and his well-dressed, well-drilled company must have made an impression in Cambridge, for most of the volunteers in camp had no uniforms, no discipline, no idea of order at all. In every way the situation in Cambridge was one grand muddle. Hundreds of men had gathered in helter-skelter fashion to fight a war that might not take place, that had no commanding officer and little in the way of arms and ammunition. On the one hand, there was danger that the British might break out of Boston at any minute and stage another battle. On the other hand, if the Americans took any action, there was danger of starting a war which might still be avoided. Certainly an attack on Fort Ticonderoga would be an act of aggression, yet the Committee of Safety had already considered this very act. Only a few months before, they had sent John Brown from Pittsfield, Massachusetts, to

Canada to size up the situation there. In his report this representative had specifically recommended an attack on Fort Ticonderoga. And now here was a man offering to make the attack.

While committee members tried to decide what to do, they gave Benedict Arnold and his company the job of delivering to the British the body of one of their soldiers who had been killed at Lexington. This would indicate to the British that the colonists did not consider themselves to be officially at war. At the same time, when the British saw Captain Arnold and his smart-looking company, they would understand that Americans were not only ready to fight but that they were not the country bumpkins the British supposed.

In the end Benedict Arnold's professional behavior impressed both the British and the Massachusetts committee. On May 2 the committee gave Benedict ten horses, one hundred pounds, a small supply of ammunition, permission to raise four hundred men, and official orders to proceed to Fort Ticonderoga. In addition, Benedict Arnold was promoted from a captain to a colonel, skipping the intermediate rank of major altogether. He couldn't have asked for more.

What the newly appointed colonel did not know was that on the same day a group of Connecticut men joined by a contingent from Massachusetts were meeting at Bennington (in the present state of Vermont) with Ethan Allen, leader of a militant group known as the Green Mountain boys. They were planning their own attack on Fort Ticonderoga.

chapter
· 3 ·

THE GROUP OF EIGHT WHO HAD started out from Hartford for Fort Ticonderoga had no difficulty in finding support. John Brown, one of the first to join up, would certainly have been enthusiastic since he had gone to Canada and proposed taking Fort Ticonderoga in the first place. John Brown's good friend, Colonel James Easton, and fifty men from the Pittsfield militia were easily persuaded to come along too. They all agreed that Ethan Allen (formerly of Connecticut) was the man to take charge.

For years Ethan and his faithful corps of Green Mountain Boys had been waging an unofficial war with New Yorkers over land claims in what would eventually become the present state of Vermont. So Ethan Allen knew how to fight, he had support, and he was acquainted with the territory. A tall man with a flashy style, he dressed in a green jacket with enormous gold epaulets and carried an oversized sword at his side. He wasn't much on drilling or the fine points of military procedure but he didn't need to be. When he was ready to go, he just said, "Come on, Boys," and his men, backwoods farmers, came along. They would have followed him to China, if that was where he was going.

It's a wonder that Ethan Allen hadn't already tried to take Fort Ticonderoga. It was the kind of adventure he jumped at and when Ethan received an invitation to join others already on their way to the fort he was ready. Strapping on his huge sword, he gave his summons. "Come on, Boys!" he called. One hundred thirty Green Mountain Boys went with Ethan, which brought the total contingent, including others picked up here and there, to two hundred thirty men.

By May 8 they had made their final plans. One of the Connecticut men, posing as a woodsman in need of a shave, had been allowed inside the fort to visit the barber. On his return he had reported that there were not more than fifty British at the fort and no one suspected an attack. So the date was set, May 10. The combined forces would cross the lake by boat, climb the cliff on the other side, and simply take the fort by surprise—perhaps without even a battle. Ethan Allen, who had been elected field commander by a unanimous vote, went ahead to the staging area to make arrangements. Some men were sent off on special assignments; many stayed behind at a tavern in Castleton (25 miles from the fort) to await further orders.

It was here that Benedict Arnold found them. When he heard that another group was preparing an independent attack, he was, of course, in a hurry to

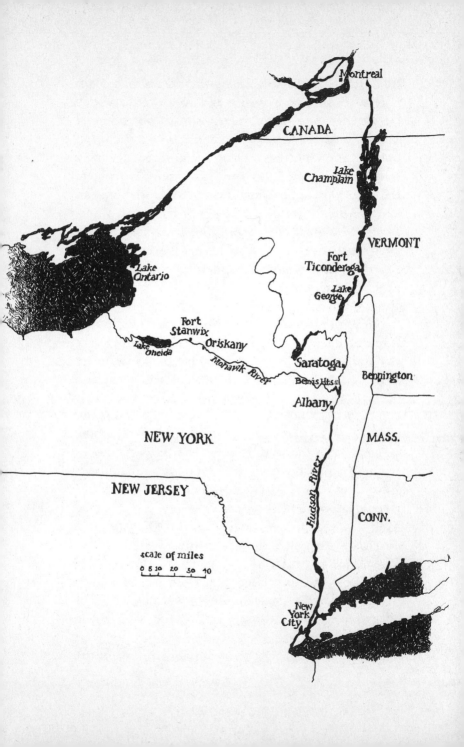

Montreal

CANADA

Lake
Champlain

VERMONT

Fort
Ticonderoga

Lake
George

Lake
Ontario

Fort
Stanwix
Oriskany

Lake
Oneida

Mohawk River

Saratoga

Bemis Hts.

Bennington

Albany

NEW YORK

MASS.

NEW JERSEY

CONN.

Hudson River

scale of miles
0 5 10 20 30 40

New
York
City

track them down and take over. He told his own unit to round up recruits and follow when they could; then he and his valet galloped north alone. When he reached the tavern at Castleton, Benedict opened the door and faced a roomful of noisy frontiersmen, laughing and drinking. These were the men he was seeking, he was told, so Benedict adopted his most military manner. He was Colonel Arnold, he informed them in his loud voice. He'd been sent by the Massachusetts Committee of Safety to capture Fort Ticonderoga. He held up his official orders. He was now in command, he announced.

For a moment the Green Mountain Boys simply stared at Benedict and at each other. It wasn't every day they saw such a sight. A brash bantam rooster of a man, dressed up and playing soldier, waving an official-looking paper, proclaiming he was their commander. And the man with him—who was he? Well, he was a personal servant, it turned out, come along to keep the colonel neat. The Boys grinned.

One man in the room, however, was not amused. John Brown was married to a cousin of Benedict Arnold's. Moreover, as a student at Yale, he had lived in New Haven, so he already knew a great deal about Arnold and what he knew he didn't like. Right from the first, he was angry. How, he asked himself, had a Connecticut man been able to wangle orders from the Massachusetts government? After all, John Brown told himself, this attack had been *his* idea in the first place.

Indeed, from the point of view of all those

present, Benedict Arnold's claim to command seemed preposterous. In those days men generally enlisted with an officer of their choice or they elected their commander, as the New Haven company had elected Benedict. And Colonel Arnold had appeared without a single recruit. The Green Mountain Boys informed the Colonel that they had a duly elected commander, thank you. Ethan Allen was his name. And they would serve under no other.

When Benedict asked to see Ethan Allen, he was taken north to the staging area. Ethan, who had no official orders, had more respect for the Massachusetts papers than the others had, but before he could say a word, the Green Mountain Boys stacked their muskets. They would go home, they said, rather than serve under anyone else. That settled the matter. Even Benedict saw that there could be no attack without the Boys. Still, Ethan Allen didn't like to reject that Massachusetts paper altogether. So he told Benedict he could come along. They would enter the fort side by side. Later Benedict wrote that he'd been given a joint command (which he may have), but in *his* report Ethan Allen never mentioned Benedict at all.

In any case, when they crossed the river in the early hours of May 10, Benedict Arnold in his red jacket and Ethan Allen in his green one were in the same boat. They climbed the cliff together, each making sure the other did not get ahead. Together they led the way into the fort, where all was quiet. Ethan flattened a sentry with the side of his sword and on the parade ground the Boys leveled their guns at the barracks.

"Huzzah! Huzzah! Huzzah!" they shouted. That should waken the British, they thought, and show them who was in charge.

Meanwhile Ethan ordered the sentry, back on his feet now, to lead the way to the officers' quarters. Up a flight of stone steps, side by side, Ethan and Benedict pounded. At the top Ethan shouted for the commanding officer.

"Come out of there, you damned old rat!"

A door opened and an officer, half dressed, his breeches in his hand, rushed into the hallway. He was only a junior officer, but Ethan and Benedict did not know that.

Ethan commanded the officer to surrender the fort.

"By what authority," the officer asked, "do you assault a British fortress?"

Ethan Allen recognized a historic moment when he saw one. "I come," he cried, "in the name of the Great Jehovah and the Continental Congress."

He could hardly have named higher authorities, but the junior officer seemed unimpressed. He didn't even put on his breeches. Actually he couldn't have done much. Any official action was up to the commanding officer but he was in his room quietly and thoroughly getting dressed. He was putting on his full dress uniform, buckling on his sword, making sure he appeared at his formal best. When he finally emerged, he looked at the tall, green-coated American and at the short, red-coated one, both of whom were shouting at him to surrender. The officer walked to the window that overlooked the parade ground. When he saw that his men had been rounded up and were being held at gunpoint, he handed his sword to Ethan Allen. It was all over. Fort Ticonderoga, with its cannon, its ammunition, and its arms, was in the hands of the colonists—Massachusetts, Connecticut, the Green Mountain Boys. It wasn't clear to which of these it belonged, but at least it was no longer in British hands.

At the moment all the Green Mountain Boys cared about was celebrating their victory. They found 90 gallons of rum in the storehouse and the only thing they could think to do with so much rum was to drink it. So they drank and went on a wild rampage of destruction: breaking up furniture, taking property from the prisoners, throwing things about. In an attempt to establish order, Benedict Arnold shouted, he commanded, he threatened, he cited military law, he waved his official papers. He did everything but shoot, but the Boys just laughed and shoved him out of the way. No cocky little colonel was going to spoil their fun. Indeed, they were all so sick of seeing Benedict Arnold's papers that the Connecticut men wrote up an official-looking document of their own and gave it to Ethan Allen so he'd have something to wave back at Benedict.

Although Benedict himself had never shown great respect for higher authority, he demanded respect from others. As usual, he made enemies.

John Brown, who took the news of the capture of
Ticonderoga to the Continental Congress, became a
lifelong enemy and did not hesitate to let Congress
know what he thought of Arnold. His good friend,
Colonel Easton, whose rank Benedict refused to
recognize, became such an outspoken enemy that
eventually Benedict "kicked him very heartily" and
ordered him off the post. But Benedict Arnold
could not simply shout and kick his way into the
command of the fort. The final decision was up to
the colonies, but which colony? For the next six
weeks first one order, then another, arrived at the
fort, each contradicting the last one. Yes,
Massachusetts wrote, Arnold was in charge. No,
the next report came. Massachusetts had handed
over the command to Connecticut, which had
originally supplied most of the money. Since there
was no central authority and no formal war, the
colonies had mixed feelings about taking responsi-
bility for the action at Fort Ticonderoga, yet all
agreed that the fort must be kept.

For practical purposes, however, Benedict
Arnold was actually in command for a brief period.
Many of the Green Mountain Boys went home after
the fort had been taken; their job was done and they
had farms to tend. And when Benedict's New
Haven unit of fifty arrived on May 14 in a captured
British vessel with an additional fifty recruits,
Ethan Allen reluctantly agreed that Colonel Arnold
could have the command, temporarily at least.
Besides, Ethan was busy writing letters, trying to
get support for a full-scale attack on Canada itself.
Later he would go to the Continental Congress to

promote the idea. Meanwhile Benedict wasted no time in sailing the captured vessel to the British garrison at St. Johns on the northern part of Lake Champlain. Surprising the British, he took the garrison and captured a large sloop with two brass cannons on it. With this success behind him, he settled down to his command—supervising every detail from cutting trees to baking bread. He was in the midst of his busy schedule when Colonel Hinman from Connecticut arrived with one thousand men to take command of Fort Ticonderoga.

Benedict could not believe that such a thing could happen. In fact, he refused to believe it until the Massachusetts government sent a committee to confirm it. On June 24, the committee said yes, Colonel Hinman was now in command. Colonel Arnold was second in command.

Second? Benedict Arnold would be second to no one, he declared. Massachusetts shouldn't have given him the job if they didn't trust him. He could not or would not understand that the decision was a political one and had nothing to do with him personally. He just knew that he was outraged; his honor had been questioned. So he resigned on the spot and took his recruits with him. Furthermore, since Massachusetts thought so little of him, he wondered if he shouldn't return the captured sloop to the British. He was speaking sarcastically in the heat of the moment, but unfortunately John Brown either heard him or heard of the remark. In any case, he didn't forget.

Altogether it was a bad time for Benedict Arnold.

He was suffering from gout and when he arrived home in New Haven, Hannah met him with the news that his wife had died the week before. Hannah was taking care of the children as she would continue to do. As for the business, she said, it was at a standstill. Discouraged, saddened, and in pain, Benedict went to bed. The first thing he had to do was to recover from his attack of gout; then he could start putting the pieces of his life back together.

The political situation had changed since he'd left New Haven in April. The Battle of Bunker Hill had been fought on June 17 and although the colonial forces had run out of ammunition, just as they had expected, they killed one thousand British soldiers first. (The Americans lost only four hundred men.) Openly at war now, the American forces may have been short of supplies of all kinds, but they had at last acquired a commander-in-chief. General George Washington was in Cambridge, trying to bring order out of chaos, trying to make plans for the future. Surely, Benedict Arnold thought, there would be a campaign against Canada. And surely he could play a leading role in it. As soon as he was better, he would go to Massachusetts, collect the money that was owed him for the Fort Ticonderoga expedition, and then become an officer in the new Continental army.

So at the end of July he presented his bill to the Massachusetts congress—about 440 pounds, which he claimed he'd spent out of his own pocket after running out of Massachusetts money. The members of the congress looked over the bill and shook their heads. Too much, they said. Here he was charging them for blankets when blankets had been supplied. And what about food? Where had he listed the specific items of food he'd bought and how much each had cost? Well, there was no such record. Benedict Arnold had not made a notation every time he'd bought a barrel of flour. He didn't bother with such details either in his private or his public life, but nevertheless he insisted that he knew how much he'd spent. Didn't the Massachusetts congress believe him? Benedict bridled as he always did when he felt his honor had been affronted. But Massachusetts cared nothing for his honor, only for his accounts. When they paid him, they gave him less than half of what he'd asked. (A year later the Continental Congress agreed the payment had been unfair and made up the difference.)

Benedict Arnold was sick to death of squabbling and bickering with what he considered petty-minded men. It was all he'd been doing for the last three months and now he longed for some grand venture to throw himself into, body and soul. Perhaps he indicated as much to General Washington when they met. In any case, the two men did meet and took to each other immediately. Washington admitted that Colonel Arnold had a "tincture of vanity" about him, but he recognized a fearless soldier when he saw one. And that was exactly what Washington needed. He was planning a two-pronged invasion into Canada—one force going up Lake Champlain to Montreal, the other force marching overland through the Maine wilderness and emerging on the banks of the St. Lawrence River opposite the city of Quebec.

Benedict Arnold was made a colonel in the Continental army and was given the command of the wilderness part of one campaign.

chapter

· 4 ·

BENEDICT ARNOLD NOT ONLY reveled in the actual physical activity involved in a campaign, he was inspired by the idea of heroism. He liked to think of himself in terms of past heroes who had been in similar situations, so now, assigned to capture the city of Quebec, he cast himself in the role of General James Wolfe, the most famous and best loved hero of the French and Indian War, the man who had captured Quebec for the British and had died in battle. Indeed, who but a hero could take such a city? Situated on a sheer, black slate cliff 300 feet above the St. Lawrence River, Quebec was protected by hills, moats, ditches, walls; it was locked behind gates. Yet Arnold dreamed of mounting that cliff, battering the walls, entering one of those gates, and becoming a hero just like the illustrious Wolfe. Of course he had one advantage over Wolfe. Like many others, he believed that when the Canadians had the opportunity, many would rush to the American side. He even took handbills with him, inviting the Canadians to come and "range themselves under the standard of General Liberty."

But first the Maine wilderness had to be crossed. The fact that no one knew much about the wilderness did not seem to bother Benedict Arnold. He had a map and a journal kept by a British engineer who had made the trip fifteen years before, and though there were, as Arnold figured, about 180 miles to cover, most of it was by water: up the Kennebec River, across a 12-mile stretch of land (known as the Great Carrying Place) to the Dead River, up that river for 30 miles, across another 4 miles of land to a stream, then to a lake, and then to another river which finally emptied into the St. Lawrence 4 miles from Quebec. The most difficult part would be carrying the boats and supplies across the connecting strips of land, but even this did not look too hard. There seemed to be ponds to break up that long 12-mile stretch across the Great Carrying Place. In any case, one did not expect great victories without hardship. So Arnold sent a rush order to Maine for two hundred bateaux, heavy flat-bottomed boats, to carry his army and its provisions through the waterways of the wilderness. The expedition, he predicted, would take about twenty days.

On September 19 his army of 1,051 men, packed into eleven vessels, sailed from Newburyport, Massachusetts—colors flying, drums beating, fifes playing. There were riflemen dressed in ash-colored hunting shirts, musketmen with feathers in their hats, and leading them all in a topsail schooner was Colonel Arnold, wearing a great plume in his cocked hat. Among Arnold's officers was a frail-looking nineteen-year-old by the name of Aaron Burr. He'd been in bed in Cambridge with what was called a "nervous disorder" when he'd heard of the expedition and determined to join it. His friends had told him he'd never survive; his uncle refused to let him go, but Aaron pointed out that there was no way anyone could stop him and no one did. In addition to the men, there were two wives who went along and a number of dogs, including Captain Dearborn's large, friendly Newfoundland.

On September 24 at Fort Western (now Augusta), 30 miles up the Kennebec River, the army held a frolic and a barbecue to celebrate their last night in civilization. After filling up on three bears, roasted corn, cake, rum, and cider, they sang hearty songs and probably felt cheerful in spite of the unknown hazards that might lie ahead. They knew that they would likely have problems with the boats. The two hundred bateaux that Colonel Arnold had ordered were poorly constructed and made of green wood. When Arnold protested, the carpenter explained that he'd never had an order for so many bateaux at one time; besides, green wood was all that there was available. So the boats had been patched up, loaded with provisions for forty-five days, and now stood ready to set out the next morning. All anyone could do was to hope for the best.

No one, however, had counted on the rivers

being so difficult to navigate. At times the current was so swift the men had trouble making any progress at all, even though they used both oars and poles at the same time. At especially bad spots, they had to lean out of the boats, grab hold of bushes on the banks and pull themselves forward inch by inch, from bush to bush. Sometimes they had to jump overboard and push the boats over rocky bottoms. "You would have taken the men for amphibious animals," Arnold wrote. Indeed, both the Kennebec River and the Dead River ran wild and unreasonable courses: twisting and turning; running now deep, now shallow over rocky bottoms; boiling up into rapids; and suddenly dropping off into waterfalls. Of course the boats (weighing about 400 pounds each) had to be carried around each waterfall. The cargo had to be carried too—100 tons of supplies, too much to be moved all at once, so the men had to go back and forth, back and forth each time. As it turned out, there were seventeen falls.

The men cursed the rivers and they cursed the boats, not only because they were heavy and unwieldy but because they leaked. By the end of the first two weeks water seeping through seams and cracks had spoiled the fish they carried, the bread, the salt, the beef, and the dried peas. All had to be thrown away. One oarsman, frustrated at every turn by the wretched boats, wrote in his journal that he wished he could come "within reach of the villains who constructed these crazy things."

By the time they came to the Great Carrying Place, eighteen of the twenty days that Arnold had calculated for the journey had gone. One hundred men had dropped out because of sickness or plain discouragement; the rest had run out of all food except flour, a pint of which was doled out daily to each man. "A little water stiffened with flour" was what they ate, one man wrote. Moreover, the weather had turned cold.

In Washington's orders to Arnold, he had provided for unforeseen difficulties and hazardous weather. "In that case," he had written, "you are to return." But Benedict Arnold, who was at his best when pushed by physical challenge, never considered turning back. Riding in a canoe for quick passage, he ranged up and down the river, encouraging his troops, urging them on, reminding them of the glories that lay ahead with the conquest of Canada. The fate of the country rested with them, he said. All of Canada would fall if only they could manage to keep moving a little farther . . . a little farther . . . a little farther until things got better.

But nothing did get better. At the Great Carrying Place, the actual carrying became a nightmare as the land flung up one obstacle after another: hills, woods, swamps, mud, floods. Once the ground was so wet and soggy that the men had to sit up all night beside a fire in order to keep even partially dry. Sometimes they sank knee-deep in mud as they struggled along, weighted down by boats and barrels. Yet they managed to keep up their spirits. "How do you like your washing and lodging?" one mud-covered soldier would call to another.

The ponds that were interspersed along the Great

Carrying Place afforded little relief. One pond was choked with roots and all but impassable. The water in another was yellow and brackish and made the men sick. After leaving the third pond, one weary young man noted in his journal that this was the twenty-fourth carrying place.

Many of the men, perhaps because they were convinced that they were on a historic mission, kept journals.

October 19. "Cooking has gone out of fashion," one officer wrote as provisions gave out altogether.

October 21. A tempest of hurricane strength flooded the country, turning a river which had been 60 yards wide into a lake which was 200 yards wide. "This was one of the most fatiguing marches we had . . . having no path and being necessitated to climb the steepest hills and that without food."

October 25. Snowstorm. Lt. Colonel Enos and his men turned back. There were only seven hundred men left now.

October 28. Abandoned the boats. "With inexpressible joy we dropped these grievous burdens."

October 29. Slept under four inches of snow. Although the men were reduced to eating candles, soap, and hair grease, one man had a small piece of luck. "Good fortune!" he wrote. "Killed a partridge."

October 30. Soup was made by boiling deerskin moccasins, roots, and bark. "No one can imagine . . . the sweetness of a roasted shot-pouch to the famished appetite."

October 31. Captain Dearborn's Newfoundland dog was killed. "I sat down on the end of a log," one soldier wrote, "absolutely fainting with hunger and fatigue." He was given a cup of broth made from the Newfoundland. Jemima Warner, one of the two wives who had come along, buried her husband under a pile of leaves, put on his cartridge belt, picked up his musket, and marched on.

As the situation became increasingly serious, Arnold and his aides rushed ahead to an Abenaki Indian settlement on the St. Lawrence in the hope of finding provisions. On November 2, when the men had reached the very end of their endurance, a line of cattle arrived, enough so that each man could be allowed a pound of meat. Meal, mutton, tobacco followed quickly. "When we saw the cattle that Arnold sent," a soldier reported, "it was the joyfulest sight I ever beheld, and some could not refrain from tears."

On November 9, after forty-five days and 350 miles of travel from Fort Western, six hundred men out of Arnold's original army reached the St. Lawrence River—"a band of scarecrows," one man wrote, "resembling the animal called the Ourang-Outang." That they had survived at all was proof of their great courage. That they were still willing, even eager, to attack Quebec was proof of Benedict Arnold's strength as a leader. He was both admired and liked; yet as usual he had also made enemies. One officer from Connecticut resented the brutal way that Arnold had reprimanded him on one occasion. Aaron Burr thought Arnold "had provided too carefully for himself" on the march. The Abenaki Indian chief, Natanis, called Arnold "the Dark Eagle" and predicted his future. "The Dark Eagle will soar aloft to the sun," he said, "yet when he soars the highest, his fall is the most certain."

The other prong of the Canadian expedition under General Richard Montgomery had had its difficulties too. Confrontations with the enemy. Shortages of food. Bad weather. But perhaps worst of all was the uncooperative attitudes of the army itself. The New Yorkers and the New Englanders did not get on well together and none, according to Montgomery, were easy to command. "The privates are all generals," he complained. If they didn't agree with an order, they would, likely as not, just refuse to carry it out.

Ethan Allen, who served under Montgomery, had not even waited for orders. On an advance scouting mission with a band of thirty men, he had suddenly decided just to go ahead on his own and take Montreal. He talked John Brown, who was on a similar mission, into helping him and together they arranged to cross the river on the night of October 24, each group approaching a different end of the town. Brown's men were to give three huzzahs as the signal for a joint attack. But Ethan never heard the huzzahs. Perhaps John Brown thought that the weather was unfavorable; perhaps he just decided that the plan was crazy. In any case, he never showed up. Instead, English and Canadian troops surrounded Ethan's little band at the lower for ammunition that when the Canadians fired their cannons into the Plains, the Americans would run to pick up the balls for their own use, waving their thanks to the enemy. After a few days Arnold saw that he would have to retreat up the river and wait for reinforcements from General Montgomery. As it happened, Montgomery had taken Montreal on the same day as Arnold had made his attack on Quebec. Aaron Burr, disguised as a priest, went to Montreal with the message.

Two weeks later (December 2) Montgomery arrived with three hundred men and a large supply of ammunition, food, and winter clothes. Fortunately General Montgomery, who had fought with Wolfe, was one of the few men whom Arnold did not mind serving under. So together they proceeded to the outskirts of the city and Montgomery tried, as Arnold had, to induce the Canadians to surrender. He wrote threatening letters, suggesting how strong his forces were, how dangerous it would be to resist. When the letters were rejected, he tied new letters to arrows and shot them over the city walls. They were ignored. So there was no way out. The Americans would have to storm the city.

But before they could even start, there were difficulties. Reinforcements arrived to strengthen the Canadians. Smallpox broke out in the American camp. Even among those who were well, there was trouble. Some of the men whose term of enlistment was up at the end of the year balked at risking their lives now. Three officers decided to form their own company with Major John Brown as their leader. It end of town and Ethan Allen became a prisoner of the British.

Just as Ethan Allen had to set his dreams aside, Benedict's dreams were being put to the test. On the night of November 13 he began his move on Quebec. He landed his men in what was known as Wolfe's Cove and proceeded, just as Wolfe had, to the broad fields known as the Plains of Abraham behind the city. First he tried to persuade the Canadians to surrender without a fight. Now would be a good time, he figured, for liberty-minded Canadians to defect. But when Arnold sent a messenger with a flag of truce to the walls of the city, the flag was shot out of the messenger's hand. When Arnold sent another flag, it was shot down too. When he tried, like Wolfe, to lure the Canadians into the open to fight, he got nowhere. The Canadians stayed behind their walls.

As it happened, if Benedict Arnold had known all the facts, he might have taken the city by surprise when he'd first landed. According to an account of a participant, one of the gates to the city was unlocked that night and the key had been lost. On the other hand, if the Canadians had known how few Americans there were and what a small supply of ammunition and arms they had, they might have come out of their fortress and won the battle then and there. Apparently Arnold himself did not realize how badly his supplies had been damaged by water. Each man, he discovered, had only five rounds of cartridges and just one man in every six had a musket that worked. So desperate were they took some spirited talking to overcome these pockets of resistance, but General Montgomery, described as "a gentle, polite man," was also firm and persuasive. In the end he inspired the men to stick together and make one last all-out effort to conquer Canada.

In order to surprise and confuse the enemy, the Americans waited for a snowstorm to make their attack. The snow came on the night of December 30 and when they started out, each man wore in his hat a slip of white paper marked with the words "Liberty or Death." The white papers were meant to keep the men from mistaking each other for the enemy, but the snow turned into a driving blizzard which promptly destroyed the papers and all but blinded the men. Montgomery's men, marching in single file, slipped and fell and slipped again as they tried to climb the ice-covered cliff on one approach to the city. Arnold's men, heads bent against the weather, ploughed through deep snow, holding their guns under their coats in an attempt to keep them dry as they came from the opposite side. But long before any of them reached the city, church bells were ringing and up and down the streets the cry was heard, "Turn out! Turn out!" As soon as the Americans were within range, they were fired upon. They must have realized that death, not liberty, lay ahead for many of them, yet they fought no less fiercely. Indeed, they persisted as if their will alone could subdue those terrible cliffs and withstand the gunfire. The men fell, they got up, they fired, they fell again, but somehow they kept the battle going. It was not a case of a few men performing extraordinary deeds. Every man was a hero that night.

But they did not take Quebec. Montgomery was shot in the head and killed. Arnold was hit in the leg by a bullet as he attempted to break through a barricade. He tried to go on but became faint from loss of blood. Leaning against a wall, he called to his men, "Rush on, brave boys!" And his men rushed on. They fought for three nightmarish hours before they were stopped and even then Daniel Morgan, who had taken command in Arnold's place, would not surrender his sword. He stood adamant, his back against a wall, tears of frustration running down his cheeks as he insisted he'd never turn his sword over to those "cowards." In the end, however, he did give it up, not to the "cowards" but to a priest who happened to be present. Now with the battle over, the score stood: 426 Americans captured, 60 killed or wounded; 5 British killed, 13 wounded.

Still, Arnold, recuperating in a captured hospital outside the city and back in command since Montgomery's death, did not intend to give up. Nor was he expected to. Congress made him a Brigadier General (which he considered only his due) and promised him reinforcements. "I will never leave this proud town," he declared, "unless I can first enter it in triumph."

But winter turned into spring and promised reinforcements only trickled in. By the middle of March Arnold had only 617 men and 400 of these either had smallpox or had been given an inoculation against smallpox, which meant that they were sick with a milder form of the disease. In April the number of troops increased to 2,000 but during the next month 1500 of these became sick, died, were discharged, or deserted. By this time, however, General David Wooster, Arnold's old enemy from New Haven, had taken over at Quebec, and Arnold was not only second in command, but was, according to his account, being so thoroughly ignored that he was useless. So he got himself transferred to Montreal in May and was there when a British fleet of fifteen ships (filled with eight regiments and 2,000 German mercenaries) came sailing up the St. Lawrence River.

America's chance to conquer Canada was gone. Benedict Arnold fumed at Congress for being slow and incompetent. He fumed at the stupidity of other generals. He could have taken Quebec, he insisted, if he'd been given the chance. As it was, like the rest of the army, he had to withdraw from Canada. He was the last man to leave. On the bank of the river, he got down from his horse, took off his saddle, and shot his horse in the head so the enemy wouldn't get it. Then he stepped into a waiting boat and pushed himself off.

chapter
· 5 ·

BY THE FIRST WEEK OF JULY
what remained of the American army which had
fought in Canada was back at Crown Point, New
York, just above Fort Ticonderoga. John Adams, a
member of the Continental Congress, described the
army as "disgraced, defeated, discontented, dis-
eased, naked, undisciplined, eaten up with vermin."
Yet much depended on that army. Only the week
before a massive British fleet carrying a total of
32,000 soldiers and 10,000 seamen, had begun
sailing into New York Bay. The real danger now
was not just that New York City might fall but that
one part of the colonies might be sealed off from the
others. If the British from New York were able to
sail up the Hudson River to Albany and if the
British from Canada were able to sail down the
Hudson River to Albany, all of New England
would be shut off by itself, unable to cooperate in
the war. This was what Americans had always
dreaded. So now Washington with only 19,000

poorly armed soldiers was going to try to hold New York while Major General Horatio Gates was to take command of that pitiful northern army and try to fend off the British from Canada.

At the moment, however, the men in the northern army were so busy quarreling with each other, it didn't seem possible that they would have energy left to fight the British. Even when the news reached them that independence had been declared, the men cheered but didn't act as if they felt any more united than they had before. The Pennsylvania troops (who considered themselves southerners) and the New England troops were camped on opposite sides of the lake to keep them from killing each other. "Hi-yah, no-'count Yankees," the Pennsylvanians would call to the New Englanders whenever they were within shouting distance. "Hi-yah, lousy Buckskins!" the New Englanders would call back. Junior officers wrote letters to Washington about all the mistakes their generals were making. Even the generals had difficulties. General Schuyler, who had been first in command at Albany, did not think that Gates was meant to replace him whereas Gates thought he was (and so Congress intended). It was an unfortunate misunderstanding, the beginning of a fierce jealousy between the two men, but for the time being they accepted Congress's verdict (a reversal of its original order): Schuyler first, Gates second.

And of course General Arnold had his share of trouble. John Brown was striking at him again. "General Arnold and I do not agree very well,"

Brown had written his wife from Quebec. This was such an understatement that his wife must have smiled, for although Brown was not ordinarily a hating man, he hated Arnold with a hatred that twisted his life. In some ways Brown was rather like Arnold. A natural athlete, he had become famous at Yale for his ability to kick a football over the elm tree on the college campus, and in the army he had become known as a stubborn fighter, a strong leader eager to take on daring missions. On his scouting expeditions in Canada he had exposed himself to the bitter cold for such long periods that his eyesight had been affected. There were times when he was almost blind. But it was not his eyesight that he held against Arnold. He had other grievances that he had collected during the Quebec campaign.

First, there was the matter of his promotion. Because of his spectacular capture of a British fort in the early days of the Canadian expedition, General Montgomery had promised him a promotion. But when Brown, after Montgomery's death, had asked General Arnold for that promotion, he had been refused. Arnold claimed that John Brown had been "publicly impeached" for stealing from the baggage of prisoners of war. Even General Wooster, when he took command, refused Brown his promotion. But it was Arnold whom Brown blamed. It was Arnold, he claimed, who was spreading lies about him.

Nor was this all. If General Arnold had handled the smallpox epidemic differently, John Brown's brother, Jacob, might still be alive. Arnold did not take proper measures to keep the disease from spreading. What was worse, he authorized the use of inoculation, Brown claimed, which was against orders. Actually men often inoculated each other, no matter what the orders were. In one company men blindfolded themselves for the inoculation so they could say they didn't know they were disobeying orders. Inoculation was such a controversial issue that many towns, including Pittsfield (Brown's hometown), had voted to make it illegal. Brown was obviously against it and blamed Arnold for its having been practiced in the army at all. Although an inoculation usually caused only a mild form of the disease, it could and sometimes did kill a patient and, indeed, may have killed Jacob Brown.

In July John Brown was given his promotion by Congress and his name was cleared but this did not satisfy him. He wanted to bring Arnold down. Perhaps he had personal reasons within the family, but certainly he wanted Arnold to pay for having slandered his character. Indeed, there was no area, according to Brown, in which Arnold was not guilty of some kind of misconduct. He had kept food from part of the army, he claimed; he had interfered with orders from superior officers; he had stolen from merchants during the evacuation of Montreal; he had permitted inoculation against smallpox; he had made treasonous threats at Ticonderoga. Brown forgot nothing but before he could draw up an official list of complaints,

Benedict Arnold was threatened from another quarter.

It happened during the court-martial of Brown's friend, Colonel Moses Hazen, charged by Arnold with allowing property for which he was responsible to be plundered. During the trial Moses Hazen, instead of just defending himself, accused Arnold of stealing goods from the merchants of Montreal. When the court allowed Hazen to continue his attack, Arnold lost his temper. After all, it was Hazen, not Arnold, who was standing court-martial, and Arnold didn't mind telling the court what he thought of it. The court was angry with Arnold for interfering with its proceedings. He was undermining military justice, the court declared, and it demanded an apology. When Arnold refused, the court ordered his arrest, but at this point General Gates stepped in and dismissed the court. There was a war going on, he pointed out. General Arnold was needed to command a fleet to oppose the British on Lake Champlain.

Although both General Gates and General Schuyler wrote to Congress, expressing their confidence in Arnold's integrity, Arnold felt his honor had been wounded. It was "extremely cruel," he said, to be called a robber and a thief when he had sacrificed "my ease, health and a great part of my private property" for his country. This would be his standard defense on all occasions. He seemed to imply that anyone who had sacrificed for his country could not possibly be guilty of wrongdoing. Even to accuse such a person was to show a lack of gratitude and perhaps even a lack of patriotism. Yet the fact that Moses Hazen, a Canadian who had joined the American army, had made considerable sacrifices did not seem to impress him.

But Benedict Arnold was not one to sulk if there was a chance to fight. And as commander of the fleet on Lake Champlain, Arnold would certainly have to fight if the British attempted to sail down the lake to the Hudson River. He would have to fight General Carleton, in command of the British in Canada, and he would also have to fight "Gentleman Johnny" Burgoyne, that high-handed, big-talking general who had laughed at America's fighting ability. Just let *him* go to America, he'd bragged, and he'd cross the country "with a hop, step and a jump." Of course Americans longed to trip General Burgoyne while he was hopping, but at the moment there seemed little chance to do this. Arnold's fleet consisted of just four vessels and five hundred men. "I hope to be excused," Arnold wrote his superiors, "if with five hundred men, half naked, I should not be able to beat the enemy with seven thousand men, well-clothed." But Arnold was always excited by the idea of trying to achieve the impossible. The higher the odds against him, the more eager he was for the risks. It was as if he spent his life looking for mill wheels to jump on. So now he threw himself into the business of building a fleet.

It was a race for time. At the northern end of the lake the British were building and rebuilding their fleet. Since large boats could not navigate the ten miles of rapids above Lake Champlain, the British had to knock down three of their larger vessels and put them together again below the rapids. From England they had brought precut parts of ten gunboats that had to be assembled. Smaller boats had to be carried overland around the rapids.

At the southern end of the lake, the Americans, urged on by General Arnold, were madly cutting trees, sawing wood, driving nails, raising masts. Obviously professional carpenters and blacksmiths were needed for this work. So they were sent for— to Massachusetts, Connecticut, Rhode Island, and Philadelphia. When they wouldn't come for army wages, they were paid whatever they asked. The order was: just get them. And tell them to bring their own tools. So two hundred carpenters were hard at work on the shores of Lake Champlain, trying to turn out a fleet in a couple of months.

General Arnold also needed experienced seamen to man the boats and gunners trained to lay guns. And he needed warm clothes for all his men. He didn't get the seamen or the gunners and got only part of the clothes, but by the end of the summer he did have a fleet of sixteen vessels. Gates warned him that he was to fight a defensive war and avoid "wanton risk and unnecessary display." Once on the water, however, Arnold could not help but think that he made a pretty display, all sails billowing on their way to meet His Majesty's navy. He sailed farther from Ticonderoga than Gates had anticipated, finally anchoring his fleet on September

23 in a narrow bay between the western shore of New York and Valcour Island. In case Gates should think he'd gone too far, he wrote that he was in a good defensive position with his ships arranged in a semicircle and so hidden that they wouldn't be seen by the enemy until they had sailed past. Gates approved the plan, although he did not yet understand that there was no way to prevent Benedict Arnold from taking wanton risks.

Indeed, it seemed that risk might be imperative. While waiting for the British to appear, Arnold received the news that Washington's forces had retreated and that New York City was now in the hands of the enemy. Arnold's reaction was contempt. Washington's men must have become "panic-struck," he said. "Is it possible [that] my countrymen can . . . hesitate one moment between slavery and death?" Plainly the entire strategy of keeping the British from controlling the Hudson River depended now on Arnold. And he was not one to become panic-struck.

Yet when the British fleet appeared on the morning of October 11, General Arnold was surprised. The British had twenty-nine fighting vessels with a total of fifty-three guns as opposed to thirty-two on the American side. Arnold, however, was not counting guns. In his flagship, *Congress,* at the center of his little semicircle, he was too busy giving orders, manning guns, figuring out his tactics as the British, having finally sighted the Americans, had hauled up and were trying to maneuver themselves into a fighting position. Fortunately for

Arnold, the wind was against the British and only seventeen of their gunboats were able to row into the narrow channel. Now with only 350 yards between the two lines, the two sides began their battle.

Cannonballs ripped into hulls, tore down rigging, churned up the water, hit men, wounded them, killed them. The decks were slick with blood. Though they were sprinkled with sand again and again, they remained slick. Benedict Arnold seemed hardly to notice. Limping as a result of his wound in Quebec, he scrambled over the bloody decks, aiming first one cannon for an untrained gunner to fire, racing to another cannon, then back again. Dodging shattered rigging, bracing himself against the shock of cannonballs crashing against the vessel, he shouted encouragement to his men. At the end of the afternoon one of the larger British vessels which had been held back by the wind and prevented from taking part in the battle was able to swing into position and fire broadside at the American line.

That was the end of the fighting for the day. The British anchored their fleet in a line between the southern end of the island and the mainland, waiting for morning to make the final kill. And indeed it seemed that the Americans had no alternative but to surrender. Three-fourths of their ammunition was gone; sixty men had been killed or wounded; two ships had been lost; the rest were damaged and sails hung in tatters. Still, Benedict Arnold could not picture himself handing over his hard-won little fleet to the British. Surrender? He refused to think of it.

As night came on, a thick fog gradually crept across Lake Champlain, settling like a blanket over the two fleets, and Benedict, that master of daredevil escapades, saw his chance. He gave orders that his fleet should slip quietly, one by one, through the fog, past the enemy line. No voice was to be heard, no light was to be lit except for one small hooded lantern at the stern of each vessel which would act as a guide to the boat that followed. And so they slid by the enemy, undetected, one vessel after the other, with Arnold in the *Congress* bringing up the rear. As soon as they were out of earshot, the men brought out their oars and rowed desperately toward Fort Ticonderoga.

They didn't all make it. When the fog lifted the next morning and the British found the Americans gone, they took off in angry pursuit. The wind favored them and by mid-morning they had caught up. Five of Arnold's vessels managed to get away safely. Two were in such bad condition, they were evacuated and deliberately sunk. One ran aground, one was burned by the British, two were captured. But for two and a half hours the *Congress* and four gondolas kept right on fighting as if they really had a chance against the enormous power massed against them. In the end Arnold gave up but he wouldn't surrender. He beached the five vessels and ordered them to be blown up. The last man to leave his post, he lined up his men on the shore so they could watch the boats go down, unconquered, their flags still flying. Only when the last boat had disappeared did General Arnold and the remaining two hundred men leave the scene to begin their long walk to Fort Ticonderoga. As for the British, they decided it was too late in the season for a full-scale offensive, so they sailed back to Canada for the winter.

By the next spring people generally appreciated the fact that Benedict Arnold had delayed the invasion of the British from the north. But at the time there were mixed reactions to what he had done. General Gates called Arnold's defense "gallant" and said, "Few men have met with so many hair-breadth escapes in so short a space of time." General William Maxwell at Ticonderoga wrote that "Arnold, our evil genius to the north, has with a good deal of industry got us clear of our fine fleet." John Brown added another black mark to Arnold's crimes, charging him with "misconduct of the Continental fleet in Lake Champlain."

But to the average patriot, discouraged by the bad news from Washington's army, Benedict Arnold, whether he'd lost or not, seemed like the hero that they were looking for. And when he stopped home on his way to his next assignment in Rhode Island, he was given a hero's welcome. Parades marched, cannons were fired, townspeople huzzahed, including all those former neighbors who had predicted that he would turn out badly. Certainly he appeared a hero to his sister, Hannah, and to his three sons: Benedict who was eight now,

Richard who was seven, and Henry who was four.

Gratifying as attention might be, however, Benedict Arnold could not just sit still and enjoy it. He had to be doing something. Before going on to Rhode Island, he organized an artillery regiment which cost him a thousand pounds of his own money. Of course he expected Congress to repay him, but as always, he was casual about money. He spent grandly, impulsively, generously. Indeed he didn't like to think about money although he was forced to dream up schemes for getting it. He wasn't particular about the kind of schemes; he simply got money any way he could. He had learned this as a merchant during the days of the Sugar Act. A practical businessman took advantage of whatever opportunities were present. When there weren't opportunities, he borrowed.

During the next four months Benedict Arnold did a great deal of spending. General Washington had asked him to make sure that the British anchored off Rhode Island were only wintering there and not planning an invasion. He suggested that Arnold might raise troops in Boston, which he proceeded to do. A pleasant task, it turned out, for while he was in Boston, Benedict Arnold fell in love.

He met Betsy De Blois at a party given by General Henry Knox. Betsy was sixteen, a Tory, beautiful, and talkative. In a satire about Boston society, she was referred to as Miss Volubility, but Benedict Arnold did not care how much she talked as long as she talked to *him*. The best way to impress her, he thought, was to spend money. So he bought her a whole trunkful of fashionable silk and satin dresses, and since he did not want to neglect his own wardrobe, he bought himself a sword knot (a fancy tassel attached to the hilt of a sword), a sash, epaulets, and a dozen pair of silk hose.

Benedict Arnold was thirty-six years old now, and for a while as he swished about Boston with his new sword knot and sash he felt, in the words of that Indian chief in Quebec, that he was truly "soaring." But then everything seemed to go wrong at once. Betsy refused to accept the trunkful of dresses. She decided that she preferred another man to General Arnold—a younger man, a druggist just as Benedict had once been. It was as if Benedict Arnold had turned himself into a great general for nothing.

Then the troops he had expected to take with him to Rhode Island were transferred to Fort Ticonderoga. Apparently no one considered the British presence off the coast of New England a danger now, so Benedict went back to Rhode Island, frustrated at every turn. The war seemed to be going on every place except where he was. He had not even been invited back to join the northern army in which he felt that he belonged. And then he received the most devastating news of all. Five officers had been promoted to major general and they were all his juniors. He had been the next man in line for promotion and Congress had passed right over him.

This was a "civil way," Arnold said, "of

requesting my resignation. When I entered the service of my country, my character was unimpeached. I have sacrificed my interest, ease, and happiness in her cause."

Indeed he could see no way of retaining his honor and continuing in the army. This was a common attitude among military men who felt slighted, and throughout the Revolution officers often resigned if they were passed over. But in Congress John Adams had little sympathy for military men with sensitive natures. He was sick of officers who quarreled "like cats and dogs." If they had virtue, he said, they would continue in service, whatever their rank. If not—well, let them retire and good riddance.

John Adams was reflecting the civilian point of view. Many people were afraid that military men might become so powerful, they wouldn't want to give up their power after the war was over. Americans were fighting to get rid of a king and they didn't want to end up with a military dictator. They knew that this could happen and had happened, for people at this time believed in the importance of understanding history. So they insisted that wartime power must remain strictly in the hands of civilians. Congress would decide which officers would be promoted. Although their length of service (their seniority) would be considered, it would not be a deciding factor as was traditionally the case in armies. Merit would also be a consideration. In addition, Congress would take into account the number of senior officers who came from each state. In the case of Benedict

Arnold, Congress explained, he had not been promoted because Connecticut already had two major generals.

"I confess," George Washington wrote to Arnold, "this is a strange mode of reasoning." Strange or not, however, General Washington understood the civilian point of view and accepted it as a political fact of life. Benedict Arnold, on the other hand, had difficulty understanding any but his own point of view. Bravery was what he knew; rewards and admiration were what he expected. And no matter what explanation Washington offered, Arnold was convinced that Congress had been influenced by lies that had been spread about him. He demanded a court of inquiry, but as Washington pointed out, no charges had been made against him. "I do not see upon what ground you can demand a court of inquiry." Always a firm supporter of Benedict Arnold, he tried to soothe him. He offered to give him a command in the Hudson Highlands where the Americans were trying to build up their defenses. In particular, they were concentrating on "the West Point," an S-shaped curve in a narrow section of the Hudson River north of Bear Mountain. Arnold did not accept the assignment. He intended to go to Philadelphia and hand in his resignation—that is, if Congress didn't change its mind.

Yet in early April when his duties in Rhode Island came to an end, he did not go directly to Philadelphia. Instead, he went home to New Haven where he fretted and fussed over his predicament. He could not picture himself as a civilian with a war raging around him. Men riding into battle while he stayed at home! Yet his honor was at stake. What could he do?

Meanwhile John Brown was still conducting his campaign against Arnold. Ever since the preceding September, he had been trying to get Benedict Arnold to stand trial for his alleged "misconducts." He had gone from "generals to Congress and Congress to generals," he said, but no one took notice. In disgust he resigned from the army and had a handbill printed, listing all his old accusations against Arnold and ending up with a charge so shocking, so extravagant that people simply didn't believe it. "Money is this man's god," Brown wrote, "and to get enough of it, he would sacrifice his country." The handbill was printed on April 12, but before a copy reached Arnold, the war intervened.

At three o'clock on the morning of April 26 there was an urgent knock on the Arnolds' door. Outside in the pouring rain a militiaman stood, breathless with news. Two thousand British soldiers had landed near Norwalk, Connecticut, he said. They were at this very instant marching inland. General David Wooster had sent for Arnold. Would the General come?

Would he! At that moment Benedict Arnold did not care what his rank was. He didn't even care that old General Wooster was now in command of the militia and would be in command over him. Quickly Benedict put on his uniform. He jumped on his horse and was off at a gallop.

chapter
· 6 ·

THE BRITISH WERE ON THEIR way to Danbury, a major arsenal and supply depot for the American army. For some reason, perhaps due in part to the heavy rainstorm, Connecticut residents were slow in responding, so the British marched the twenty miles from the coast without trouble or interruption. By the time General Arnold and General Wooster, with a party of five hundred hastily summoned men, reached Bethel (two miles from Danbury) it was too late. The town was in flames and there was nothing they could do. Still, they had no intention of letting the British off free. The next day they would fight them on their way back to Norwalk. Wooster would attack from the rear; Arnold would meet the enemy head-on as they approached.

Long before daylight Arnold and three hundred men were on their way. At Ridgefield Arnold picked the battle site—a spot where the road was squeezed between a rocky ledge on one side and a big farmhouse on the other. With the help of local residents, Arnold's men piled furniture, wheelbarrows, wagons, carts, lumber across the road to form a barricade. When they were done, Benedict Arnold, astride his horse, took a position in the center of the road behind the barricade and waited. As soon as he heard firing, he knew that Wooster had attacked. It would be his turn next.

Then down the road came the British. An unending column, three abreast. Tramping, tramping as if nothing would or could stop them. And what could? Three hundred men against two thousand. And only a ramshackle barricade between them. Anyone would have said the American position was impossible, but then Benedict Arnold thrived on the impossible. As soon as he went into action, he became alive as he was never alive except in danger. Indeed, he made himself at one with danger. He turned into someone other than himself, more than himself, and who could say now what was possible and what was not?

Many of his men, however, were not as inspired by the impossible as he was. Still, they fought on, even when cannonballs ripped into their midst, even when the British broke through their flimsy barricade. But when the enemy appeared on top of the rocky ledge and began pouring bullets down upon them, they decided they had had enough. As they retreated, Benedict Arnold, sitting tall on his horse, became a perfect target for the soldiers on that rocky ledge. Benedict was not hit, but nine bullets went into his horse. And when the horse fell, Benedict fell too, his foot caught in the stirrup, his face flat into the bloodied ground. When he looked up, a well-known Tory was standing over him, his bayonet drawn.

"You are my prisoner," the Tory announced.

In a lightning move Benedict whipped out his pistol. "Not yet," he said. He shot the Tory. Then Benedict struggled to his feet and joined his men, who had taken refuge in a wooded swamp.

This was not the end. The next day when the British arrived in Norwalk, there were Arnold and his men lined up and waiting. This time it was the Americans who took the offensive, with Benedict Arnold out in front, leading the charge. But his men could see the outcome before they had gone far. They were outnumbered and outgunned, just as they had been the day before, and in the harbor British ships were already sending boats to help the men on shore. What was the use of going on?

When Benedict Arnold discovered that his men were no longer following him, he did what no military man in his right mind would dream of doing. He turned his back on the enemy and the full force of their gunfire while he talked. He commanded his men not to desert him; he begged, he scolded. He reminded his men of their duty to their country; he spoke desperately about freedom. But nothing he said made any difference. The fighting was over. The British got away. True, they had lost at least sixty men (some said two hundred), but they had carried out their mission successfully. Ammunition, arms, tents, clothing, five thousand barrels of beef and pork had all gone up in smoke.

As for the Americans, they lost twenty men, including General David Wooster. But why hadn't they done better? Americans asked. Why hadn't Connecticut been able to act faster? Where were their men? The country regarded the whole affair as a disgrace; yet despite everything, Benedict Arnold not only came out alive, he emerged as a hero.

A personal triumph was just what Benedict needed. His confidence restored, he rode to Philadelphia, certain that Congress would be so impressed by his performance, it would give him the rank he was due.

And Congress was impressed. Within a week it made him a major general. But not the ranking major general, not the first among those who had been promoted. He was at the bottom of the list, his seniority ignored. Four other major generals who should have been below him were his superiors. Benedict Arnold would not stand for this. If he was to be recognized, he wanted to be fully recognized.

There must be an explanation, he reasoned, for the prejudice against him. By this time he had received a copy of John Brown's handbill and blaming everything on John Brown, he presented the handbill to Congress and asked for a court of inquiry so his name might be cleared. It was unfair, he said, "that having made every sacrifice of fortune, ease, and domestic happiness to serve my country, I am publicly impeached (in particular by Lt. Col. Brown)."

As it turned out, no one took John Brown's

handbill seriously, Congress gave it to the Board of War who said it was obviously so full of "wicked lies," it wasn't worth a court of inquiry. The Board listened to the testimony of Arnold and a witness he called but it didn't even bother to question Brown. The Board simply reported that General Arnold's character had been "cruelly and groundlessly aspersed."

Arnold assumed that now his rank would be restored. But no. Instead, Congress gave him a horse "as a token of their approbation of his gallant conduct" in Connecticut.

Arnold may have been pleased, but he was not satisfied. A new horse to replace one which had been killed was not much of a token, especially since he would probably have billed Congress for the horse in any case. Not that this would have done much good. Arnold was already having difficulty with Congress about his accounts in the Quebec campaign. He was running into the same kind of trouble as he had over his Ticonderoga expenses. He demanded repayment of money he'd spent but for which he had no record. In some cases when Congress checked with people to whom Arnold claimed to have given money, the people denied receiving it. Why hadn't Congress given him a paymaster, Arnold asked, if it wanted such strict accounting? He'd been forced to act as his own paymaster and he charged Congress a thousand pounds for the service.

In the end, however, as far as Arnold was concerned, it all came down to a matter of honor. If

Congress refused him a single cent of what he asked, he considered that his honor had been challenged. And "honor," he said, "is a sacrifice no man ought to make." But Congress did not grant him every single cent. It allowed him more than he could prove having spent but less than he had asked for.

John Brown's comment was —where had Arnold got so much money to spend if he hadn't stolen from the merchants in Montreal? Brown was smarting from the Board of War's dismissal of his handbill; they had made him look like a liar, he said. Indeed, he was as angry at Congress as Arnold was, but he had resigned from the Continental army. Arnold was just worrying about resigning as he talked about honor and dreamed of brave deeds and rewards. Bravery was the only way that Benedict Arnold knew to prove himself. So in June when General Washington asked him to lead a unit of untrained militia to the Delaware River, he accepted quickly.

The British were moving toward Philadelphia and Arnold was supposed to keep them from crossing the river. Or at least help to delay them. He wasn't equipped to do anything dramatic nor was he expected even to cross the river. Still, there was no chance to be brave with a river between him and the enemy, so he wrote Washington, asking permission to go after the enemy. He wanted to attack the main British army with his little corps of uninitiated recruits. "Fight them we must," he said. Although Benedict had never experienced victory, he had such an enormous sense of power that he longed to exercise it, victory or not. Besides, he was desperate to prove himself again.

Washington, however, was interested only in victory and wrote back a hasty "no" to Arnold's request. As it turned out, the British changed their minds in any case. They went back to New York City and Benedict returned to Philadelphia, where he took up his worries just where he'd left off. From day to day he postponed his resignation, hoping that Congress would reconsider and raise his rank.

It was not easy for Benedict Arnold to watch the war go on without him, particularly now that the British were embarked on a major offensive. General Burgoyne had taken over the command of the British army in the north and was already proceeding toward Fort Ticonderoga. The British were obviously hoping to do what they had failed to do the year before: take control of the Hudson River and divide the colonies. General William Howe, commander-in-chief of all British forces in North America, had his headquarters in New York City and was expected to move up the Hudson to Albany as Burgoyne moved down to join him. That is, if they had their way. The Americans pinned their hopes on the defense posts they had erected at strategic points on the river and on the construction they had built at "the West Point," that looping neck of the river in the Hudson Highlands. In an attempt to block the river itself, they had stretched a great iron chain across it. In front of the chain they had built an obstruction of logs and below the chain on the river bottom they had sunk structures with long iron spearheads designed to puncture the hulls of any vessels that might try to sail past. Guns were mounted on both sides of the river for further protection.

Americans hoped, however, that General Burgoyne would be stopped in his tracks at Fort Ticonderoga. Although Benedict Arnold and Ethan Allen had taken the fort with ease, it was still regarded as the "Gibraltar of the North," a stronghold that could withstand almost any attack. What most people did not know, however, was that Fort Ticonderoga was desperately undermanned— only twenty-five hundred soldiers, one-fifth the number that was needed for its proper defense. Moreover, Mount Defiance, southwest of the fort, remained unprotected. The hill was so steep, so rugged that the Americans in command took for granted that no one could drag a cannon up those slopes. Yet just the year before Benedict Arnold, still limping from his Canadian wound, had climbed the hill and warned General Gates that it needed a defense. If he were the enemy, he said, he would have been able to get a cannon to the top.

And when the time came, the British were also able to get cannons to the top. "Where a goat can go, a man can go," a British general said, "and where a man can go, he can drag a gun." On July 5, 1777, the American defenders at Fort Ticonderoga saw that the British had established a battery on the top of Mount Defiance. Already at a disadvantage, the Americans knew that if they were to save themselves, they would have to get out. That night they secretly evacuated the fort, leaving behind seventy cannons, food, tents, boats—all for General Burgoyne.

When New Englanders received the news, they were horrified. "Had the enemy fought and conquered the fort, I could have borne it," Abigail Adams wrote her husband, John, in the Continental Congress. "How shall our lost honor be retrieved?"

Many blamed General Schuyler, who was in command of the northern army. New Englanders had never liked him, not only because he was a New Yorker but because he was an aristocrat and haughty. Now some even suspected him of being secretly in sympathy with the enemy.

While the British were taking over Fort Ticonderoga, Benedict Arnold was finally writing out his letter of resignation, but the letter was hardly out of his hands when he heard the bad news about Ticonderoga. Along with the news came a request from General Washington. He wanted General Arnold sent immediately to join "the northern department."

Benedict Arnold swung right into action. Forget his resignation, he told Congress. Just set it aside for the time being. "No public or private injury shall prevail on me to forsake the cause of . . . my country." After he had gone north, members of Congress voted again on restoring his rank; again they voted it down. The only reason it was voted down, one disgusted member declared, was because Arnold had asked for it. Congress did not want to set a precedent. If one military man got his way by insisting on it, then all military men might think they could do the same. Congress would show once and for all that it made the decisions, and it alone.

Yet it was the military men who fought the war and right now they were concentrating on stopping General Burgoyne who was boasting that he would eat his Christmas dinner in Albany. What he did not seem to appreciate was that there were many meals between July and Christmas. In order to eat any of them, he had to keep a line clear to Canada so supplies could reach him and he had to raid the American countryside for food. He expected, however, to control much of the countryside, for he had sent Colonel Barry St. Leger with eighteen hundred men (over half of them Indians friendly to the British cause) down Lake Ontario and up the Mohawk valley to Albany. Here, according to Burgoyne's plan, they would all meet for a merry Christmas: Burgoyne, St. Leger, and General Howe who would be coming with his forces up the river from New York.

On July 24 Benedict Arnold, joining his old friend General Schuyler, set about making everything as hard for the British as he could. When Burgoyne with his seven thousand soldiers, his forty-eight pieces of artillery, his long van of carts (thirty were filled with "Gentleman Johnny's" personal belongings—clothes, silver service, wines and other comforts) marched through the woods

south of Fort Ticonderoga, he found all kinds of
obstacles in his path. Americans had been there
first: tearing down bridges, blocking roads,
jamming creeks with boulders, removing all food
and transport from the area. It was hard enough to
march across such rough land, each man carrying
sixty pounds of equipment on his back, but
Burgoyne was further handicapped because he had
too few horses, too many camp followers (five
hundred women and children tagged along), and
carts that were poorly made. His army was lucky if
it could advance a mile a day.

His fine plan for a Christmas party in Albany was
not going well at all. At the end of July General
Howe decided that Burgoyne didn't need his help
in taking the Hudson. Since he had done so well at
Fort Ticonderoga, he could undoubtedly get to
Albany alone. Leaving General Sir Henry Clinton
in charge in New York, Howe set sail for
Chesapeake Bay with the main body of his army.
He wanted to take Philadelphia and he believed this
was just the time to do it. Moreover, he had
received permission from England to go ahead with
his plan. But Burgoyne had also received permission for his plan. If these two plans seemed
contradictory, those in charge in England did not
appear to realize it. Howe did not even check with
Burgoyne; he just told Clinton that if trouble
developed up the Hudson, perhaps he could lend a
hand.

But Howe would not be in Albany for Christmas
dinner. As it turned out, neither would Colonel St.
Leger. In the middle of August just as he was

approaching Fort Stanwix (east of Lake Ontario), St. Leger's large Indian contingent was frightened off by terrible stories of Americans who were coming to butcher them. Benedict Arnold was responsible for the stories. Sent to defend Fort Stanwix, he had with him a thousand men and Yan Host Schuyler, who was well known as a simple-minded fellow with strange behavior. Indians throughout the area regarded Yan Host as a kind of prophet in close touch with the Great Spirit. Arnold asked him to deliver a message to the Indians in the British camp. Tell them, Arnold said, that the Americans were coming. Tell them that there were more Americans than there are leaves on the trees.

Wild-eyed and screaming, Yan Host ran into the Indian camp. He showed the Indians his jacket which he'd deliberately shot through with bullets. The Americans were just behind him, he cried. Thousands of them. And with them was General Arnold, known to the Indians as "heap fighting chief." The Indians ran and since the British could not hope to beat the enemy without the Indians, they ran too. Within a week Colonel St. Leger's forces were back in Canada and Johnny Burgoyne's army was headed for Albany alone.

While the British were losing their support in the north, the American army was gaining men every day. Stories of Indian atrocities were alarming the countryside and militia from all nearby states were rushing to help defend the north. John Brown, now an officer in the Massachusetts militia, attacked a British base on Lake George and destroyed its supplies. General John Stark of New Hampshire, who had resigned from the Continental army when he'd been passed over for promotion, went back into action when the British marched into Bennington (Vermont) on a raiding expedition. Assisted by local militia and the Green Mountain Boys, Stark not only won the battle, he captured four British ammunition wagons, 250 swords, and hundreds of muskets and rifles. The British lost 900 men—207 killed, the rest taken prisoner.

With luck running against him, General Burgoyne might have turned back, but he insisted that he did not have that choice. His orders were to force his way to Albany, he said, and in spite of the fact that there actually was some flexibility in his orders, he maintained he had to do exactly as he'd been told. He had to continue to Albany and in order to get there he had to cross the Hudson River, preferably well to the north of Albany, where the river was narrow and easier to cross than it would be farther south. So on September 13 he took his army of six thousand on a bridge of boats across to the west side of the river. Once there, he dismantled the boats, which meant that his regular supply route to the north on the east side of the river was cut off. He had enough food to feed his army for just thirty days but he had no way to get more food unless he received help from the south. Obviously he had no time to waste.

Twelve miles to the south of Burgoyne's army the Americans lay in wait. Their fortifications were already built on Bemis Heights, a three-hundred-foot plateau between the river and a woods. But now the Americans had a new commander in the north. General Schuyler (dismissed by Congress because of the loss of Ticonderoga) had again been replaced by General Gates, who had become so suspicious of his old rival that he imagined that even Schuyler's friends were plotting against him. (And indeed many of them were.) Gates had always liked Arnold but as he watched Arnold taking up with former aides of Schuyler, he gradually withdrew his friendship. Although Arnold must have known why Gates had become cool, he never thought of himself as being tactless or imprudent. His friends were his own affair and he would choose them as he pleased.

In any case, Gates and Arnold, so basically different in temperament, were almost fated to become enemies once they were in battle. Right from the first General Gates had planned to take a defensive position against the British when they advanced. Let them throw themselves against the American fortifications across the river road, on the plateau, in the woods, Gates said. Time was on the side of the Americans. If the British could be held back for a month, their rations would be gone.

But of course such a conservative operation seemed cowardly and ineffective to Benedict Arnold. Let "Granny Gates" (as the men called him) fight his war safely from his headquarters in the rear. Benedict Arnold wanted to attack from the woods, where the Americans could carry on the kind of guerrilla warfare they knew best. Then when they came into the open, Benedict would ride at the head of his men, daring the whole British army, proving himself again and again. He would show Congress what kind of fighter he was; he would show General Gates; he would show the country. Then who could deny him the full recognition he deserved?

But on the morning of September 19 when the British made their appearance in a clearing around a farm owned by a Mr. Freeman, Benedict Arnold, who longed to charge right into battle, was standing in front of a red frame house which served as General Gates's headquarters. He was arguing about battle plans. General Gates wanted to stick to his defensive strategy. Arnold wanted to attack. He wanted to risk everything; he wanted to *go*. Gates said No. Arnold felt his power welling up within him, but still Gates said No. At least, Arnold begged, let him send some of his men forward. Eventually Gates agreed to this. Since the men were part of Arnold's left wing, Arnold gave the orders, but he did not go along. He directed them from headquarters, where he was told to stay. So Arnold listened to guns that were being fired a mile away. He pictured the progress of the battle from reports that were brought to him from the front. He gave his orders through the intermediary services of a messenger. When the Americans appeared to be in trouble, he ordered reinforcements but Gates countermanded his orders. Against all his natural inclinations, Arnold held himself back. Rooted to the ground, he became more impatient, more restless, more indignant.

For three hours the battle raged. The Americans and the British took turns rushing into the clearing to attack, then retreating to the woods that stood behind each army. But there came a point during the long hours when Benedict Arnold could stand it no longer. "By God, I'll put an end to it!" he cried and he jumped on a horse and galloped off. He did not go far. General Gates sent one of his aides galloping after him with orders to return. And Benedict returned. Not meekly, but he did return.

At the end of the day when darkness finally stopped the fighting, both armies claimed a victory, yet there was really no victory at all. Only dead and broken bodies strewn over a battleground: 600 dead or wounded British; 320 Americans. Burgoyne had captured a piece of farmland but the river road to Albany was still firmly in the hands of the Americans.

The fighting was not finished except perhaps for Benedict Arnold. After the Battle of Freeman's Farm, both Arnold and Gates seemed deliberately to look for ways to insult each other. According to Arnold, Gates "huffed" him daily. But when young Richard Varick, a former secretary to General Schuyler, publicly defied Gates, Arnold immediately appointed Varick to his personal staff. When Gates sent Congress his report of the battle, he omitted any mention of Benedict Arnold, although it had been his wing of the army that had done much of the fighting. When Arnold complained, Gates called Arnold's attention to the fact that he had resigned from the army. As soon as General Lincoln arrived, Gates said, Arnold would no longer be needed. Arnold asked for a pass to Philadelphia and was given it. Yet he did not leave. General Lincoln arrived and still Arnold did not leave.

"Conscious of my own innocence and integrity," Arnold wrote Gates, "I am determined to sacrifice my feelings, present peace and quiet to the public good and continue in the army . . . when my country needs my support."

His letter was ignored. Still Arnold stayed on.

When American officers signed a petition asking Gates to allow Arnold to remain through the next battle, Gates agreed but on one condition only. Arnold would take no part in the battle.

chapter
· 7 ·

BOTH ARMIES SPENT THE DAY after the Battle of Freeman's Farm burying their dead and rescuing their wounded. On the following day both armies received good news. The Americans learned that John Brown had captured Mount Defiance and the outworks of Fort Ticonderoga, along with three hundred prisoners. Although the stone fortress itself remained in British hands, Americans now had a good chance of stopping Burgoyne if he should try to retreat.

At the moment, however, Burgoyne was giving no thought to retreat. His good news came in a letter from New York. General Clinton was coming north. He would push up the Hudson, he said, with two thousand men if this would help. Burgoyne replied immediately. "Do it, my dear friend, directly." The sooner, the better. Because of his limited food supply, Burgoyne could not safely remain in his present position after October 12. Unless he had a victory before then, he would have to retreat north to look for provisions. But Burgoyne was encouraged; he might yet eat Christmas dinner in Albany. Gates would hear of Clinton's movements and he might divert part of his army south. On the other hand, if Clinton advanced far enough, Gates would find himself caught with the British on both sides.

In any case, the best thing for Burgoyne to do now was to wait. In preparation for the next conflict, he had his army build a series of redoubts—log and mud barricades behind which they could fire in comparative safety. Their largest redoubt, the Great Redoubt, extended from the bluffs of the Hudson River across the road and south toward Freeman's Farm. This was where the army camped and kept its supplies. In front of the Great Redoubt, two more redoubts were thrown up: one to the right of Freeman's Farm, one to the left.

Two miles away in the American camp General Gates was happy to wait. This had been his strategy from the beginning and he had no intention of weakening his army by sending any of it south. He knew that the British had to eat and that every day they were using up more of their food supply. Meanwhile his own army was well-fed and growing: eleven thousand men now, some of them already taking positions behind Burgoyne's lines, preparing to block his retreat. Yet rumors that Clinton was moving up the Hudson made Gates uneasy. The question was: Would Burgoyne run out of food before Clinton arrived? Or would

Clinton come in time to help Burgoyne? Perhaps even to save him?

Burgoyne was, of course, asking the same questions. By the first of October his supply of salt pork and flour, the mainstay of the army diet, was almost gone. And no word from Clinton. By October 3 Burgoyne was forced to reduce his men's daily ration by one-third; there was no food for the horses. Still no word from Clinton. On October 7 Burgoyne decided that he would wait no longer. He would fight now. By noon he had his troops in the field.

When the alarm came, General Gates was at his table, eating lunch. The main course, one soldier later recalled, was an ox's heart. In any case, the lunch was never finished. General Gates gave the order to "begin the game" and within a matter of minutes the men were called out, brigades were formed, and Americans were on the march.

Benedict Arnold was without a horse of his own since the one his sister, Hannah, was sending him had not yet arrived, so he was accustomed to using borrowed horses. At the first roll of the drum, he jumped on the back of a huge dark stallion named Warren. He intended to be ready in case General Gates had a change of heart and ordered him to the field. He watched Gates call out brigades that had formerly been under his command, but Gates never glanced in his direction. In private among friends, Arnold had been in the habit of referring to General Gates as "the Face of Clay" for, no matter what strain he was under, Gates seldom allowed any expression to cross his face. As the sounds of battle mounted, as messengers streamed back with reports and rushed out with orders, Gates remained impassive. Arnold paced back and forth on his horse but Gates gave no sign that he even noticed. All Arnold wanted was a nod. Some slight gesture that would allow him to go. It no longer mattered to him if he were in command or not. He just wanted to fight.

And Gates should have known that Benedict Arnold would eventually do what he wanted. He should have realized that when Arnold's patience gave out, there would be no stopping him. He should not have been surprised when Arnold suddenly swung his horse about. "Victory or death!" Arnold shouted. He raced headlong for the battlefield and this time he was too fast for Gates's aide to catch him.

Indeed today there was no denying Benedict Arnold. Suddenly unleashed, he threw himself totally into battle. He was a leader and he couldn't help himself; he led. When he came upon deserters, he turned them around. When he met laggers, he shouted encouragement and they ran to catch up. When he found one of his old brigades retreating from enemy soldiers, Arnold did just what he'd done at Norwalk. He turned his back on the enemy and let their bullets rain around him. "Come on, brave boys, come on!" he shouted. Not only did the Americans come on, but in short order they routed the enemy.

Like a man on fire with power, Arnold rode from brigade to brigade, giving orders to everyone, willing them all to dare, to fight, to win. Recognizing men from his hometown, he called to them. "If the day is long enough," he cried, "we'll have them all in hell before night!" The very air seemed to crackle with his presence. It was as if this were no longer an army separated into units, governed by rules. This was a body of men bound by Arnold and intent only on victory. Indeed, Arnold, galloping back and forth recklessly across the line of fire, seemed to be so completely in charge of the day, it was as if he were beyond the reach of danger. As if he were invulnerable.

Within fifty minutes of Arnold's coming on the field, the Americans had forced all the British back to their redoubts. At this point Gates might have considered the battle over. But not Arnold. He wouldn't stop. Perhaps he couldn't stop. He threw his forces against one redoubt and when it didn't surrender, he plunged on to the next. Leading his men to the sally port (or back entrance), sending them scrambling over the top of the structure, he forced his way inside. Oh, he was soaring now! Soaring as he had never soared before.

And he was cut down. His horse was shot from under him and as he went down, another bullet went into Arnold's leg. Henry Dearborn, his old friend from Quebec days, bent over him.

"Where are you hit?" he asked.

"In the same leg," Arnold replied. He must have sensed how serious his wound was. He must have guessed that his days of glory might be over. "I wish it had been my heart," he said.

The battle continued after Arnold had been carried away but only sporadically. The momentum was gone and that night Burgoyne, leaving his camp fires burning to mislead the Americans, began to retreat.

He was not sure that he wanted to go far in case General Clinton's forces might still come to the rescue. He didn't know that on that very day Clinton, having already taken two American forts in the Hudson Highlands, had broken through the log jam and chain at West Point. Nor would Burgoyne know. "Nothing between us now but Gates," Clinton wrote to Burgoyne. The note was enclosed in a silver bullet but the messenger who carried it was caught by the Americans. Although he swallowed the bullet, the Americans forced him to vomit it up. Then they hanged him as a spy. Within a few days General Gates would have the note and would know more about Clinton's activities than Burgoyne would. But, of course, no one would know what Clinton planned next.

Burgoyne's army moved slowly north, sometimes no more than a mile an hour. By October 13 he was no farther than Saratoga (now Schuylerville), but the Americans had moved quickly. All at once Burgoyne found that his army was surrounded. No matter which way he might turn, the Americans were there to stop him. He called his officers together for a council of war. Would it be honorable, he asked, to approach Gates about terms to stop the fighting? His council told him it would not only be honorable, it was unavoidable.

On October 14 British representatives spoke to American representatives and to their surprise found that General Gates had already written out his terms. Indeed, he was so quick to present them, so eager to have them completed (by two o'clock the next afternoon, he said) that Burgoyne became suspicious. Perhaps Gates knew something about Clinton that he didn't know. Perhaps Clinton was just around the corner.

Burgoyne stalled. He proposed counter terms. He objected to the word "surrender." He didn't like "capitulation" either. Burgoyne was *able* to continue fighting, he insisted; he *chose* to stop because, outnumbered as he was, he knew that further fighting would only pile up the dead on both sides.

When the new terms were offered, Gates didn't argue. He was even willing to call this agreement a "convention" instead of a "capitulation." But whatever it was, it must take place immediately. So on the afternoon of October 16 General Johnny Burgoyne handed his sword to General Gates and on the following morning the British troops laid down their arms.

As it turned out, Gates need not have hurried and Burgoyne need not have stalled. On the sixteenth, the same day Burgoyne surrendered his sword, an expedition of Clinton's forces was turned back 45 miles south of Albany. Clinton had already returned to New York City and now he recalled all his men from the Hudson.

News of the victory at Saratoga came to the

country like rain after a long drought. For months there had been only defeats and humiliations for the Americans. Washington had been beaten in Pennsylvania at Brandywine and at Germantown. On September 26 General Howe had taken possession of Philadelphia. But at last there was something to celebrate. Americans had actually captured 5,791 British soldiers—and that included 8 generals. No matter what the British called it, this was nothing less than a full-fledged, out-and-out surrender. Gentleman Johnny, with all his hopping and stepping, had jumped right into their hands. When his conquered army marched across the country from Saratoga to Boston, Americans flocked to see the sight. Nothing like this had ever happened in America before. Just watching the endless procession was almost more than Americans could take in.

Meanwhile Benedict Arnold was waging his own war. Just as he suspected, his wound was serious. A doctor had examined him while he was still on the battlefield and warned him that he might lose his leg. Benedict wouldn't listen to that kind of talk. It was "damned nonsense," he cried. If that was all the surgeon could say, he wanted to be put back on a horse and see the action through. When he was moved to the army hospital in Albany, the doctors there also insisted that his leg should be amputated. Arnold forbade it. Even the idea enraged him. He needed a whole body in order to be brave. Indeed, it was as if the doctors were suggesting that they wanted to remove his very self. Who would he be?

What kind of life could he lead with only one leg? What would be left for him if his mill wheels were taken away?

Arnold kept his leg but it healed slowly and painfully. Tied on his back to a board so he couldn't injure his mending bones, he was angry at everybody and everything. He wanted to burst his bonds, to be free, to be well. He wanted to go to Philadelphia and tell Congress that Gates should never have given in to Burgoyne's so-called "convention." Then when he heard that Congress had voted to strike a gold medal in honor of Gates, he decided again, as he had so many times in the past, that Congress did not know what it was doing. Congress had even promoted an aide of General Gates from a lieutenant colonel to a brigadier general simply because he had carried the news of Burgoyne's surrender to Philadelphia. Was that the kind of valor that Congress was rewarding now? His friends noted that Arnold continued to be very ill and "low spirited." But it was no wonder. According to Arnold, no one seemed to be doing anything right. Not Congress. Nor the army.

Not even his doctors knew what they were doing, Arnold said. "He abuses us," one of his doctors reported, "for a set of ignorant pretenders." When it was pointed out to him that General Lincoln, lying in the next room with a shattered ankle, was not complaining, Arnold was not impressed. He had never claimed to be a patient man; his strength was bravery. Strapped to his board, he railed at the world and everyone in it. "He is very weak and full of pain," a friend wrote. "He seems to be discouraged at laying in Bed so long." He was peevish.

One piece of news, however, improved his spirits for a time. On November 29 Congress instructed Washington to issue Arnold a new commission with the proper rank of major general which he'd been seeking. At last that stubborn body of men had recognized his worth. Still, he waited eagerly for the final satisfaction. Only when the official commission signed by Washington was in his hands would he feel fully redeemed. He waited for two months. He would have found no excuse for his old friend's delay. Nor did Washington offer any. He did not refer to the terrible conditions that his army was enduring in their winter quarters at Valley Forge. Nor did he mention that his own pride was suffering. Ever since Saratoga, he had been compared unfavorably to General Gates, the new hero of the day. All Washington said when he sent Arnold his commission was that up to this time he'd been without the proper forms. And he asked if Arnold would be well enough to serve in the next campaign.

Arnold waited exactly two months to reply. No, he said, he would not be well enough.

In March Arnold was moved to Connecticut on a stretcher. He went to Middletown where his children were in school and for the next five weeks he recuperated. By this time he knew that one leg was two inches shorter than the other and though he could have his shoe (all those pretty shoes!) built up, he would in a sense always be a cripple. He could look forward to graduating from crutches to a cane and perhaps one day could walk without support, but he would limp. At the moment, since there was no easy way he could be a hero, his mind automatically turned to prewar days when he found his satisfactions in acquiring money and living well. He bought a share in a large privateer, a vessel armed and commissioned to wage war on the enemy while bringing in profit to its owners.

And he wrote to Betsy De Blois. It seemed that she had not married her apothecary after all, although she had gone as far as the church. The ceremony was cut short by her mother who stood up in her pew and simply forbade the wedding to go on. Apparently Betsy had gone home with her parents and that was that. So Benedict decided to try again. He wrote his letter carefully, making a rough draft first and then copying it. "Twenty times have I taken up my pen," he wrote, but his heart "so calm and serene amidst the clashing of arms" trembled now with fear. He talked of Betsy's "heavenly image" and his own ardent "passion." "On you alone," he wrote, "my happiness depends." He was proud of his letter but it did not change Betsy's mind. She was no more inclined toward General Arnold than she'd been a year ago.

On May 1 Benedict went to New Haven to stay with his sister. He was given a hero's welcome, a thirteen-gun salute with the usual parades and displays, and though he reveled in the attention, he may have felt somewhat let down a few days later when New Haven fired its guns again and put on an even greater display. This time it was in honor of the French. Americans were celebrating the fact that France had entered the war on their side. Throughout the country the cry went up: "Long live the King of France!"

Benedict was not at all sure that he welcomed France into the war. He found it hard to turn off his lifelong prejudice and he really didn't care to drink to the long life of a French king. And why had the French decided to join the Americans? It was the victory at Saratoga, people said, that had convinced the French that the Americans could win their war. The victory that Benedict had helped to bring about. And now, Benedict asked, if Americans did win the war, might they not be dominated by the French when peace came? And wouldn't that be worse than being dominated by the British?

Sometimes he did not know what his countrymen could be thinking. But at least they were thinking of him. He received a gift from General Washington— a set of epaulets and a sword knot. Washington was eager for Arnold to join him at Valley Forge. There was news that General Howe had been recalled to England and that General Sir Henry Clinton would take his place as commander in chief of the British army. Moreover, when Howe left, he was expected to withdraw his forces from Philadelphia, so there would be action before long. Yet Washington was concerned for Arnold's health. "Don't come to camp too soon," he said.

On May 20 Benedict Arnold arrived in Valley

Forge. On May 28 General Washington, eager to give Arnold a responsible position that did not involve combat, made him military commander of Philadelphia, which had just returned to American hands.

And on May 30 Benedict Arnold took the oath of allegiance required now of all officers. "I do swear," he said, "that I will to the utmost of my power support, maintain, and defend the said United States against the said King George the Third . . . and will serve . . . with fidelity, according to the best of my skill and understanding."

chapter
· 8 ·

PHILADELPHIA HAD CHANGED
in the nine months of British occupation. Most of
the Patriot residents had moved out when the
British had moved in, leaving the city largely in the
hands of Tories and of Quakers who, because of
their peaceful religion, tried to be neutral. This was
such a congenial atmosphere for the British that
General Howe had decided he'd just settle down
and have a good time. Besides, with New York and
Philadelphia both in British hands, the war must be
almost over, he'd thought, so why not enjoy
himself? With his encouragement, Philadelphia
suddenly turned into a center of social activity—
balls, plays, dancing, parties. Had it not been for
the number of British uniforms about, a stranger
would hardly have guessed that this was a city at
war with an enemy encamped just twenty-five miles
away.

Among the many who enjoyed the pleasures of
Philadelphia in the winter of 1777–78 were two

young people whose names have survived in history only because of Benedict Arnold. Neither had met Arnold yet. In the midst of war they were playing an elaborate game of dress-up and their one object was to have fun.

Twenty-six-year-old British Major John André, who had been captured in the Canadian campaign, had recently been exchanged as a prisoner of war and was now an aide to General Charles Grey. André was a romantic young man who lived life as if he were performing roles on a stage. Before joining the army he and a select group of friends had met to read poetry aloud, to discuss beauty, to play music. They considered themselves more sensitive, more artistic, more refined than the common run of people. And indeed André was talented. He wrote poetry, painted portraits, played the flute, and enjoyed creating theatricals.

But André could play many roles. When required to take an active part as a soldier, he was proud of being a bloody one. Before coming to Philadelphia, he had, as aide to General Grey, participated in what the Americans called "the Paoli Massacre" in which two hundred American soldiers had been taken by surprise and bayoneted. Even the wounded, even those who had surrendered were cut down without mercy. This was General Grey's style. Known as "No-Flint Grey," he was famous for preferring the bayonet to the gun and young Major André felt manly and heroic following in his commander's footsteps. The sensitivity he admired in polite society had no place for him on the battlefield. His ideal soldier performed without feeling, without remorse, without question and after the grisly massacre at Paoli, John André was happy to think that he had measured up. "I must be vain enough to tell you," he wrote his mother, "that he [Grey] seemed satisfied with my service." There was only one thing lacking in his personal drama. If only he could be wounded! He didn't wish for a serious wound, he said. Just something he could brag about.

In Philadelphia, however, André, reverting to his society role, became a drawing room idol: an artist cutting out silhouettes of friends at parties, a theatrical producer staging plays, a poet turning out pretty phrases to please pretty girls. In particular, he became the darling of a group of teenage girls just entering society and giddy with the sudden attention they were receiving. Seventeen-year-old Peggy Shippen was one of the most ambitious of this group and the one whose destiny, along with André's, awaited the arrival of Benedict Arnold.

When Peggy had been born, the last of four daughters, her Quaker father had welcomed the arrival of a new baby but admitted that it was "the worst sex." Perhaps Peggy tried to overcome this handicap in her father's eyes, for she deliberately sought his companionship, tried to understand his business affairs (generally not considered to be a woman's domain), and shared his interest in politics. Like her father, she was ambitious for social position and like him too she was forever fearful that something would go wrong with her life. When anything did go wrong, Peggy went into uncontrollable hysterics. It was as if her world was so precariously balanced that at any threat she felt as if it were falling apart.

When she was seventeen, however, her greatest worry was how to wheedle enough money out of her father for a new gown. This was no small matter. Mr. Shippen worried and wailed about the state of the country and the state of his purse. He cut down on the number of horses he owned and argued with his daughters over every skein of wool they wanted to buy. Indeed, he had little choice. In order to be safe, he had to be neutral, so he refused to do business with either the British or the Americans. As a result, of course, he had little income.

But Peggy was impatient at all this haggling. Everyone knew that her father, though a Quaker and officially neutral, was sympathetic to the British and everyone must know, as she and her friends did, that the British would win. So one day there would be money. Meanwhile Peggy would be seventeen only once. Perhaps she would never again have as glamorous a social season or as many escorts. So she argued and must have been somewhat successful, for she became a model of fashion, her skirts ballooning with hoops, her hair teased and mounted so high, she had to hold her head out the window when she rode in a carriage. But Major André said that towering hair was the rage in London. And Major André, Peggy and her friends agreed, knew everything about fashion. He

helped them design their hats, took an interest in
their clothes, and charmed them with his
compliments. He gave Peggy (and perhaps her
friends too) a lock of his hair in remembrance of
their good times. (She kept it until she died.)

The most exciting time of all was scheduled to
take place in May. Planned as a farewell to General
Howe who was being recalled to England, it was to
be an extravaganza in imitation of a jousting match
of the Middle Ages. Fourteen officers dressed as
knights were to be divided into two teams which
would stage a mock battle. The Knights of the
Blended Rose would be decked out in elaborate red
and white silk costumes. Their motto would be:
"We droop when separated." The Knights of the
Burning Mountain would be in black and orange,
with the motto: "I burn forever." Also participating
in the pageant would be fourteen ladies whose favor
the knights were supposed to be seeking. Each lady
was to be dressed in a Turkish costume with a
spangled gauze turban, a veil, a white silk robe
trimmed in the colors of her knight, and a sash
edged with silver lace. Major André was in charge
of painting the scenery and designing the ladies'
headdresses. And among the fourteen ladies chosen
for the pageant were all three of the unmarried
Shippen girls. Including Peggy.

In all likelihood the British paid for the Turkish
costumes so Mr. Shippen was probably spared the
usual bargaining session. In any case, all went well
right up to the day of the festivities (May 18). Even
the weather was fair. But that morning a committee

Peggy Shippen, drawn by John André.

of Quakers called on Mr. Shippen. After they left, Mr. Shippen summoned his daughters. The committee had pointed out that the Turkish costumes were immodest. What was more, it would be unseemly for the Shippen girls to take part in such an extravagant affair intended to honor a British general. So Mr. Shippen forbade his daughters to go. He ordered the costumes returned to British headquarters and no arguments, however hysterical, changed his mind.

One month later the British left Philadelphia to return to New York. Before he went, John André, who had been living in Benjamin Franklin's empty house, helped himself to a collection of Franklin's rare books, a set of china, some musical instruments, and a portrait of Franklin. He presented the portrait to General Grey who, along with Howe, was returning to England. André was thinking of his own advancement and in due time he received it. On Grey's departure, André became aide to the commander in chief, General Sir Henry Clinton. Indeed, Major André was as eager to soar as General Arnold was. And clearly he was climbing.

But Peggy was downcast. With the departure of the British and the arrival of the Americans on June 19, she was convinced that her good times were over. Three thousand Tories had moved to New York with the British troops, and the Patriots (like Franklin's family) who had deserted Philadelphia during the occupation were coming back. Already Patriot girls, proud of their simple homespun clothes, were trying to shame Peggy and her

fashionable friends. Of course when General
Arnold rode into the city, he made it seem like a
gala occasion, but Peggy was not encouraged. She
knew the American temperament. Penny-pinching
and plain. But she did not know Benedict Arnold.

Actually a military commander should have been
penny-pinching and plain if he wanted to keep
peace in Philadelphia. Certainly he should have
been tactful, for Pennsylvania's governing body,
like the Continental Congress, was jealous of its
civilian reponsibilities and suspicious of military
control. And Joseph Reed, the dominant force in
that body, was a self-righteous, egotistical man,
eager to pounce on corruption, quick to suspect
disloyalty. If Arnold knew that he was stepping
into a delicate situation, he gave no indication that
he cared. He was not cut out to be a diplomat. He
was a hero. Yet there was no call, people pointed
out, for him to behave like a conquering hero.
Right from the beginning he seemed determined to
show Philadelphia that the British were not the only
ones who knew how to live in style. He moved into
the Penn mansion which General Howe had
occupied, bought himself a chariot and four horses,
employed ten servants, and proceeded to entertain
on a lavish scale.

Of course, to live in style he needed money but
he was well aware of the possibilities in his position
for making it. He had never been good at keeping
his public and private accounts separate and he
wasn't good now. If he acquired material for the
army and sold the surplus for his own profit, it was

hard to prove from his records that he'd done anything wrong. If he took advantage of his office to make questionable deals with New York merchants, he knew how to keep the transactions secret. If he used government wagons to transport private goods, he thought of it as "borrowing." Other influential men speculated in various ways. They reasoned that if they lost money because of the war, they had a right to get some of it back. Whatever Arnold's reasoning, he would not have admitted even to himself that he did wrong. How could he? He had given up everythng for his country; he had even become a cripple. That was justification enough for him.

Perhaps if he had been less haughty or if he had lived more quietly, Arnold would have made less trouble for himself, but he trimmed his behavior for no one. When an aide ordered a sergeant in the militia (instead of a servant) to bring a barber to the house, Arnold offered no apologies in the ruckus that followed. The sergeant, as it happened, was the son of Timothy Matock, secretary of the Pennsylvania Council and close friend of Joseph Reed, who in a series of newspaper attacks claimed that an "indignity" had been imposed on a "freeman." Arnold simply said that he was "not to be intimidated by a newspaper." When he was criticized by Reed for entertaining numerous Tory ladies, Arnold replied that he had not yet come to wage war on women.

Among the numerous Tory ladies to whom Reed objected, Arnold had almost immediately singled out one as his favorite. Eighteen-year-old Peggy Shippen was everything that Benedict admired. Beautiful, aristocratic, she shared Benedict's love of luxury and was sympathetic to his mounting complaints. Of course he was mistreated and unappreciated, she agreed. Of course Joseph Reed was a busybody and a tyrant. Of course Congress was incompetent and arbitrary. Indeed, if America won the war, she couldn't imagine how Congress could keep the new nation from falling apart. But Peggy did not think America would win. She was one of those who deplored America's refusal to consider a recent British peace offer. After all, the British had agreed to all of America's demands except the demand for independence. And what would independence mean to Peggy Shippen? Hardship, most likely. So far the Patriots had done nothing but bring her worry and hardship.

Perhaps Peggy only gradually revealed her true political sentiments to Benedict Arnold, but he was the kind of man she could easily confide in. At thirty-seven, Arnold was considerably younger than her father, yet he was of her father's generation and for some reason she found this appealing. Especially so since, unlike her father, Benedict enjoyed spending money and living well. Moreover, he was a hero. What ambitious girl would not be proud to receive his attentions? The important thing was: life was not passing her by. Peggy Shippen was dressing her hair as high as ever and at every social function in the Penn mansion she was the belle of the ball.

Benedict Arnold did not take long to decide that he wanted to marry Peggy Shippen. He informed Peggy's father of his intentions and on September 25, 1778, he wrote his first serious love letter to Peggy. He still had the rough draft of the letter he'd sent to Betsy De Blois and on reading it over, he decided he couldn't do better. So with few changes he copied it. "Twenty times have I picked up my pen," he wrote.

Mr. Shippen was not enthusiastic about the match. General Arnold was too old, he told Peggy; he had three children; he was a cripple. Moreover, there were unpleasant rumors about his financial dealings in New Haven before the war. They would wait and see, he said. While they waited, Benedict increased his attentions and multiplied his promises to Peggy. He discarded his crutches for an ivory-tipped cane, but he moved awkwardly and often required the support of an aide. When he sat, he propped up his bad leg on a campstool. Mr. Shippen worried that his leg might never heal and he told Peggy again, Wait and see. But after three months Peggy didn't want to wait any longer. Indeed, she gave the impression that waiting was bad for her health, so Mr. Shippen gave in. By January 1779, Peggy and Benedict were unofficially engaged and looked forward to a spring wedding.

But Benedict had to have more money. Many of his schemes had not worked out. He had brought Hannah and his three sons to Philadelphia and would soon be sending the two older boys to a private boarding school. Peggy would have to have an elegant house. There was no end to his need of money. But where would he get it?

In the past when things had gone wrong, Benedict had simply flung himself into action. Over the next months he thrashed around, looking for a way. He could do well at sea, he thought, even with a bad leg. So he asked Washington if he could be made an admiral, but nothing came of the suggestion. He asked Congress to be put in charge of a fleet of privateers operating out of New London. Congress turned him down.

Once he thought he might just settle down and be a landed gentleman in New York, like General Schuyler. At least New York seemed to honor its heroes. In appreciation of his part in the victory at Saratoga, New York was thinking of giving him an enormous tract of confiscated Tory land—13,000 acres, in fact. So on February 3, 1779, Arnold left for Kingston, New York, where the legislature was meeting.

On the way he was stopped by a messenger. In his absence the Pennsylvania Council had made public a proclamation in which eight charges were leveled against him. He was accused, among other things, of illegal purchases, illegal use of government wagons, improper treatment of a militiaman, and neglect of "patriotic persons" in favor of "those of another character."

Benedict did not go on to Kingston. He decided to return to Philadelphia and demand that his name be cleared in a court-martial. As always, it was the "ingratitude" of people that struck him hardest.

After all he'd done! "I daily discover so much baseness and ingratitude among mankind," he wrote Peggy, "that I almost blush to be of the same species."

After much wrangling about who should conduct the trial—civilian or military authorities, a military court-martial was finally agreed upon but no date was set. In the interval Arnold's enemies used the time to rant and rail against him. Even John Brown jumped at the chance to renew his old grievances. Of course Benedict wanted to have it over, not only to quiet the talk but because he saw this as a way to prove himself. Surely when his countrymen saw how mean-minded and ungrateful his enemies were, they would be ashamed of his treatment. Surely he would emerge as a hero again. The army knew his worth and George Washington had always been one of Arnold's most loyal supporters.

In the meantime, however, Benedict Arnold had no intention of appearing humbled before his enemies. In March he bought Peggy the elegant house he had promised her. Mount Pleasant, with its formal gardens rising from the river front, was described by John Adams as "the most elegant seat" in Pennsylvania. The estate was not available for occupancy yet, but at least (although heavily mortgaged) it legally belonged to him. Walking the grounds one day, he could not resist stopping to carve his initials on a tree trunk: B.A. It was as if the boy Benedict who had left his initials in Norwich was telling the world: Look here! See how far Benedict Arnold has gone!

On April 8, two weeks after the purchase of the house, Benedict and Peggy were married quietly at her father's house. A soldier stood beside Benedict to support him during the ceremony. Yet happy as he was, he could not have been easy. The future was too uncertain—not only because of the court-martial but because of the war itself. Now that he could no longer dream of charging onto a battlefield, the war seemed a terrible obstacle in his way. Time and again he found himself, like Peggy, wishing it were over. Settled and done with. Instead he had to stand by and watch his prospects dwindle. Money was scarce and losing its value day by day. His salary (as well as that of most officers) had not been paid for months. He could not trade; he could not fight; he had not the means to go on living as he was. He could not even say his name had been cleared. He could only wait. And Benedict Arnold was not good at waiting. He wanted to *do* something. He and Peggy must have talked about various things that he might do, but on April 20 they set aside these possibilities. On that day Washington informed Arnold that his court-martial would be held on May 1.

Benedict Arnold must often have pictured the scene of his trial. He would wear the epaulets and the sword knot that Washington had given him. He would conduct his own defense. He even knew what words he would use, but just as he was ready to leave for the trial, he received a letter from Washington. The trial had been postponed, Washington said. No other date had been set. The

Pennsylvania Council, it seemed, claimed that it had not been given enough time to gather its evidence.

Benedict Arnold did not appreciate the complicated political struggles going on behind the scenes. Joseph Reed had threatened to withdraw Pennsylvania's cooperation with Congress on all matters if this trial was not postponed. It didn't matter to Benedict that Washington was caught in the middle of a bad situation. Benedict Arnold simply decided then and there that Washington had turned against him. He was not a true friend.

He wrote to Washington: "If your Excellency thinks me a criminal, for heaven's sake let me be tried immediately and if found guilty, executed . . . For me, delay is worse than death."

It was time, Arnold decided, to investigate those other ways in which he might prove himself. If he could not win the war for the Americans, he might at least bring the war to an end. Everyone was tired of it. Everyone was discouraged at the way it dragged on and on. The British were looking for a way out, it was said, and trying to tempt American officers to change sides. And what American officer would have more influence with his countrymen than Benedict Arnold? Indeed, what normally might be considered an act of treason might actually be the highest form of patriotism. It had been so in England in the civil war of one hundred years ago. George Monk had become famous and won all kinds of honors and rewards when he changed sides and brought peace to his country. Like Monk, might not Arnold turn out to be the greatest hero of his time if he did the same? It was the kind of impossible one-man mission that was a challenge to Benedict Arnold. Moreover, such an act should be worth a lot of money to the British.

He would, of course, have to find a way to make secret negotiations, and Peggy knew how this could be done. A Philadelphia merchant, Joseph Stansbury, was a strong Tory and a friend of Major John André. He could have a pass to travel into New York City and could act as a messenger. Stansbury, described as a "nimble, sugary, obliging little fellow," agreed. So Benedict Arnold began to communicate with the enemy. He signed his name *Monk*.

chapter

· 9 ·

IN APRIL, THE MONTH BEFORE the secret negotiations began, John André, aide-de-camp to General Clinton, had been put in charge of British intelligence. This was a new role for him to play and it set his imagination spinning. He made a list of American generals who might be persuaded to change sides and dreamed up fantasies in which they would suddenly see the light and rush into the arms of the British. General Schuyler, for instance, might inspire a Tory uprising in Albany; he might even manage to turn West Point over to the British.

General Clinton did not encourage such daydreams. A conservative man, he warned André to be suspicious of all secret communications from the enemy. So when Joseph Stansbury arrived at British headquarters with a message from Benedict Arnold, who had not even been on André's list, André went straight to Clinton for advice. In his own mind he could foresee a drama in which somehow he, as an accomplice, would be thrust into an heroic part, but for all his romantic tendencies, André had a hard core of realism in his character. He never forgot that his future depended on General Clinton and he was determined to serve him well.

In this case that meant he had to follow a cautious course. How did they know that the offer really came from Arnold? Clinton asked. If it was Arnold, how did they know he was sincere? Perhaps he was really trying to get information, not give it. Keep up the correspondence, Clinton advised André. Ask Arnold to furnish them with information as it came along. As for money, no specific sum should be mentioned. They would see first what Arnold could do.

André carried out Clinton's instructions carefully. But since he couldn't create a drama, he decided that he would at least make up the stage directions for one. So he worked out a secret code for correspondence. He gave Stansbury a legal book exactly like one he had. He and Arnold would write in numbers, he explained. One number would indicate the page on which the word they wanted to use appeared. Another number would indicate the line. A third number would indicate the word on the line. And they would use invisible ink. If it was the kind that could be read when the paper was held over fire (a candle, for instance), the communication should be marked with an F for *fire*. If it was the kind that could be read when acid was applied, the letter should be marked with an A for *acid*. They would even hide the real meaning of the letter by pretending to talk of another subject—"an old woman's health," for instance. André would sign his name *John Anderson.*

Arnold was disappointed in André's reply. After all, he was no ordinary general. He was the kind who had changed the course of battles and now he was offering to win the war for the British. Yet they did not seem impressed. He'd expected jubiliation. And praise. And gratitude. And money. Definite sums of money. Although André made it clear there would be rewards, he was vague. How much? Arnold wanted to know.

Still, Arnold adopted the code, answered the letter, and a correspondence was established. It didn't always go well. Once a letter got wet and when acid was applied, the ink ran, turning the message into an unreadable smudge. Several letters, delivered now in various covert ways, were lost. Twice either Arnold or André happened to use a different edition of the code book so their letters made no sense at all. The basic difficulty, however, was that Arnold wanted to talk money and André didn't. At least not until Arnold had actually done something—provided an accurate plan of West Point or perhaps turned over a post. But Arnold needed to command a post before he could turn it over and he wouldn't be given a command until he was cleared in his court-martial. So the correspondence lapsed for a while.

Meanwhile Arnold knew that he could still change his mind. If the court-martial went well, if he came out on top, he would not need to go ahead

with the British. The trouble was that the court-
martial kept being delayed—from June to July.
Then fighting interfered and the trial was postponed
indefinitely. It did not finally take place until
December 23, 1779, in a tavern in Morristown,
New Jersey, the winter headquarters of Washington's army.

Benedict felt optimistic about the trial. Leaning
on his cane, decked out with epaulets and sword
knot, he was the very picture of a wounded hero.
Indeed, he even felt innocent. Some of the original
charges had been dismissed for lack of evidence,
and he was sure that there was not enough evidence
to convict him on the remaining counts. When it
came time for him to defend himself, he omitted
some pertinent facts, lied about others, but as usual
he concentrated on a review of his record.

How could anyone suspect him of wrongdoing?
he asked. He "had sacrificed domestic ease and
happiness . . . and a great part of a handsome
income" for his country. He was one of the first
"who had appeared in the field." He had spilled
blood. He read letters which Washington had
written praising his conduct and he reminded the
court that Congress had given him a horse in honor
of his gallantry. "My conduct from the earliest
period of this war to the present time has been
steady and uniform."

Listening to himself, Arnold would have believed
every word. In the light of his past glories,
everything else (even an act of treason) seemed
irrelevant. It was as if he put all his shining

moments on a scale and the rest of his life didn't need to be weighed at all. Benedict wasn't just acting for the benefit of the court; he *felt* like an injured hero. Moreover, he assumed that everyone must see him in the same way. So when the day came in late January for the verdict to be announced, Benedict Arnold took his seat with an air of one who expected to be congratulated.

On most counts, Arnold was acquitted for lack of evidence, but on two he was censored. He should not have made personal use of those army wagons; he should not have issued a certain illegal pass. These seemed such minor improprieties that Arnold expected them to be overlooked. Instead, the court ruled that Benedict Arnold should receive a formal letter of reprimand from General Washington. This was not a punishment; it was a humiliation. And impetuous as he was, Arnold must have wanted to resign from the army then and there. He had always talked resignation as soon as he was slighted, but now he had Peggy to think of and a baby that was expected in March. If he resigned, he would not be given a command. He would, in effect, be closing the door to future negotiations with the British. So Arnold held his temper. There was more than one way to redeem his honor. He'd renew his contacts with the British.

At the moment, however, both Major André and General Clinton were in South Carolina where the British were conducting a campaign. In desperation (perhaps at Peggy's insistence), he humbled himself and went to the new French ambassador, asking to borrow money. His argument was that he couldn't afford to stay in the army without a loan. Surely, he reasoned, the French would not want to lose the services of such an outstanding general. And surely the ambassador could not easily refuse him. Benedict Arnold had been his official host at the Grand Festival that had celebrated the ambassador's arrival in Philadelphia. Of course Benedict did not need to be told such a loan would not be proper. He knew it, yet he hoped. In spite of the fact that he hated the French, he hoped. Afterward he was sorry that he had gone. The French ambassador not only refused Arnold, he preached a little sermon on morality in public office.

The spring of 1780 was a bitter one for America. The British were winning victories in the south while Americans were having trouble even finding money to pay their soldiers. Militiamen who signed up for short stints could not be depended upon for long, serious campaigns, yet who could expect a professional army to fight without pay? General Schuyler reported that there was a "spirit of discontent . . . of alarming nature" in his area because the soldiers hadn't been paid. In Connecticut two regiments mutinied. Washington wrote that unless some system was found to pay the army, "our affairs must become desperate, beyond the possibility of recovery . . . Indeed, I have almost ceased to hope."

At the end of May, Charleston, South Carolina, fell to the British and the whole country was thrown into a state of despair. No defeat had been

as hard for Americans to take. Benedict Arnold saw
it as the beginning of the end of America's struggles
which, he said, were like "the pangs of a dying man,
violent, but of a short duration." He, of course,
expected to strike the final blow. It would be easy if
the British would only listen to him. Pay the
American soldiers enough, he argued, and they'd
quit, especially if Benedict Arnold led the way.
They'd always followed him, hadn't they? But the
British wanted a specific service, not advice, from
Arnold and during the spring Peggy and Benedict
had thought of just what they could do.

West Point. Benedict Arnold would not only
provide an "accurate plan" of West Point, he would
obtain command of the post and turn it over to the
British. Everyone had always agreed that if the
British controlled the Hudson River, the war would
soon end. But it was a peculiar twist for his life to
take. Here he was planning to give the British what
he had twice risked his life to keep the British from
getting. Yet it was a prize the British would surely
pay dearly to get.

So while André and Clinton were still in the
south, Benedict went ahead with his plans. He tried
to sell both Mount Pleasant and his Connecticut
house and convert whatever he owned into cash.
He arranged to transfer his money to London
where it would be safe. He worked at settling his
disagreement with the Treasury Board over his
Canadian expenses. He wrote General Schuyler,
asking him to speak to Washington about the
command of West Point. He even visited West

Point with its series of forts (one named Fort Arnold), its recently constructed redoubts and its new chain. In André's absence, Arnold had been feeding information to the British general who was temporarily taking Clinton's place in New York.

On June 12 Arnold wrote that he expected soon to be in command at West Point. (In fact, he had heard nothing official.) On June 16 he described the layout of West Point, stressing the weak points. It was poorly planned, he said, badly provisioned, and easily reached. The famous chain could be broken "by a single ship, large and heavily loaded, with a strong wind."

The day after he sent this message, André and Clinton arrived back in the north. André had become a major in the course of the last year, had been promoted to deputy adjutant general, and would soon become the adjutant general. He would write his mother that he could hardly look back on the "steep progress" he had made without "feeling giddy." And now as he read over Arnold's secret correspondence, the old daydreams revived. If Arnold could actually deliver West Point, André would play a leading part in the drama, one that would surely thrust him to even more breathtaking heights. Eagerly André resumed his role as John Anderson.

Arnold had given up using the name *Monk;* perhaps he thought it was too obvious. Sometimes he signed himself *Mr. Moore* or *J. Moore* (the significance of which, if any, is not known). Sometimes he used *Gustavus,* the name of a

Swedish military hero famous for his war on Catholics and his hatred of the French. (Occasionally he used the initials *A. G.*, for Adolphus Gustavus.) When he wrote now, he was insistent upon an agreement on terms. Ten thousand pounds he wanted, no matter what the outcome. In addition, an annual income of 500 pounds guaranteed for life. And finally, for turning over West Point: "Twenty thousand pounds Sterling I think will be a cheap purchase for an object of so much importance," he wrote.

André, replying to Arnold on July 23, would only go so far as to say that 20,000 pounds might not be too much for West Point if it included three thousand men, artillery, and provisions. But the other amounts "whether services are performed or not it can never be made." Even this much of a commitment, however, would have encouraged Arnold, but he did not receive the message until a month after it had been sent.

Meanwhile Arnold, for all his plans of turning over West Point, did not even have the command of it. On July 31 he was with the army at King's Ferry, New York, when he approached Washington directly and asked him about his assignment. Washington replied that yes, he had given Arnold an assignment. He was to have command of the left wing of the army. This was just the kind of assignment that Arnold would normally have loved—a chance to play an active, leading part in the forefront of battle. So Washington was surprised when Arnold was upset by the news. He never "opened his mouth," Washington reported later, not even to thank him for an assignment that any other officer would be overjoyed to receive. So sure that Arnold would be agreeable, Washington had already included the announcement in the general orders to be issued the following day.

The report reached Peggy in Philadelphia. She was attending a dinner party when a latecomer brought what he obviously thought was good news. Peggy promptly went into hysterics. Strangely enough, although she was unable to control her emotions, she never gave away secrets in these spells of hers. When one of the guests explained that Benedict's assignment was far more important than the one he had expected at West Point, Peggy became wilder than ever but wouldn't say why. The guests decided that she must be worried about the safety of her husband in such a command, and Peggy did not contradict them.

Benedict Arnold, however, had no intention of giving up West Point. When the shock had worn off, he returned to Washington and asked point-blank for the command at West Point. Limping conspicuously, he explained that he was physically unable to fight in the field. Washington gave him what he wanted. The general orders of August 3 included the correction. "Major General Arnold," the order read, "will take command of the garrison at West Point."

Arnold went immediately to West Point and by August 5 he had moved across the river from the fort into the former home of Beverly Robinson, a prominent Tory who was in New York, working closely with General Clinton. Arnold was now in the position he'd looked forward to: one man alone accomplishing the impossible. But one man alone committing treason, he discovered, was not like one man alone leading a battle. There was no one to follow. He was simply alone. Indeed, he didn't even know whether the British had decided to go ahead with the plan. Or if they would pay him. Or how much. And in this new post he had no one to carry messages to André so he could find out. He spent his time pretending to strengthen the post for the Americans while secretly trying to weaken it for the British.

All this was hard on Arnold's nerves. His leg was hurting again. His financial deals were going poorly. He couldn't sell his Connecticut house and the man who bought his china couldn't pay for it. For ready cash, Arnold resorted to filling up a spare room with food supplies from the army and selling them for his own benefit. He tried to make friends with a man from Haverstraw, Joshua Hett Smith, who seemed like a possible accomplice for future schemes, but his aides opposed the friendship. Although Smith claimed to be a Patriot, he showed such an obvious desire to be liked by everyone (particularly by the General) that Arnold's aides didn't trust him. They nicknamed him "Snake-in-the-Grass Smith" and warned Arnold to have nothing to do with him.

Everything about his present plight troubled Arnold, but in addition he brooded over old

insults. When he wrote Peggy, he lashed out at all
his old enemies but particularly at the French
ambassador whom he seemed to hate the most.
Even Hannah, who lived with Peggy and read the
letters, accused Benedict of being a "perfect master
. . . of ill nature." And, indeed, he felt ill-natured—
cross, frustrated, and lonely. He wanted to see
Peggy and little Edward (now five months old).
When would they come for a visit? he asked.

On August 24 Arnold finally received André's
letter with the promise of twenty thousand pounds.
It had probably gone to Philadelphia first and been
forwarded in a roundabout way by Peggy.
Although it was a relief to be back in
communication, Arnold still wanted the British to
meet all his original demands. The important thing
now, however, was to arrange a personal interview
to seal the bargain.

On August 30 he tried to get a letter through to
André by giving it to a man on his way from
Connecticut to New York. The letter was
addressed to Mr. John Anderson, merchant, and
was to be left with a minister in New York who had
been in on the plot from the beginning. The letter
was never delivered.

On September 3 Arnold sent another letter, this
time with a Canadian woman who was traveling to
New York with her two children. In this letter he
developed a specific plan as to how he and André
might meet. Since Arnold was in command of
various nearby posts as well as West Point itself, he
had talked to Colonel Sheldon, stationed at South

Salem, telling him to expect to hear from a John Anderson who was acting as a secret agent for Arnold. In his letter to André, Arnold explained that he should dress as a merchant, go to South Salem and Colonel Sheldon would see that the two got together.

André did receive this letter but apparently had different ideas about the meeting. He wrote Colonel Sheldon, introducing himself as John Anderson, and informed him that he would have a flag of truce and be at Dobbs Ferry on September 11 at twelve noon to meet with Arnold whom he referred to as "Mr. G————." But there was part of the letter that troubled Sheldon. "Should I not be allowed to go," the letter said, "the officer who is to command the escort . . . can speak on the affair."

How Sheldon wondered, would an American spy manage to be in league with a British officer?

When Arnold read the letter, he understood that André would, himself, be the officer, but was annoyed at his indiscretion. He tried to pass off the affair by telling Sheldon that he could not account for it either. Perhaps the letter had not been written by John Anderson at all, he suggested. Nevertheless he would go to Dobbs Ferry at the appointed time, he told Sheldon, just in case.

What Arnold did not know was that General Clinton was getting nervous about André being involved in a spy mission. He did not want André going behind the American lines, so he picked Dobbs Ferry which was neutral ground and right on the river. Moreover, Clinton did not wish

André to assume a disguise of any kind for fear that if he were caught he would be branded a spy. And he forbade him to take papers with him or to return with any. Clinton had thought of an innocent-appearing scheme that he believed could be carried out openly at noon. André in his officer's uniform would accompany the Tory, Beverly Robinson, under a flag of truce. Robinson would pretend that he wanted to talk over some business in relation to his house which, of course, Arnold was now occupying. During the course of the meeting Arnold and André could contrive to be alone and make their arrangements. No one would be taking risks.

Not knowing what was going on behind the scenes, Arnold was worried. On September 10 he dashed off a letter to André. "I do by all means advise you," he wrote, "to follow the plan [I] propose of getting to our lines by stealth."

He had no idea, of course, whether the letter would reach André or whether André would even follow his suggestions. So that night he went to Joshua Hett Smith's home across the river from Dobbs Ferry. The next morning there were several British gunboats in the river, but they were usually there, accompanying the British sloop of war, the *Vulture*, which patrolled this part of the river. Arnold, assuming that the gunboats had received instructions to hold their fire, proceeded to cross to Dobbs Ferry but had not gone far when the gunboats opened fire. No damage was done, but Benedict Arnold did not continue to Dobbs Ferry.

All day he stayed on the west side of the river and John André stayed on the east side of the river, each waiting for the other to think of some way for them to meet. Neither did. So Arnold went back to West Point and André went back to New York. It was not only difficult to make plans, it seemed; it was difficult to carry them out.

chapter
· 10 ·

ALTHOUGH BENEDICT ARNOLD was experienced in practicing deceit, he had also run much of his life openly, boldly, tactlessly, doing and saying exactly what he wanted without regard for consequences. Now he had to be acutely aware of possible consequences to what he said and did every minute. He could not be open or candid with anyone, not even with Joshua Hett Smith with whom he'd become friends in spite of his aides' disapproval. Fortunately, however, he'd soon have someone he could talk freely with. Peggy and little Edward were already on their way for a visit. They would arrive at Joshua Smith's house on September 13 where they would spend the night and Benedict would meet them there the next day.

Meanwhile Arnold prepared detailed plans not only of West Point but of the posts below. He located the weak points and indicated the favorable approaches. Remembering Clinton's stipulation that he wanted 3,000 men when he took over, he was careful to note that the total number of men under his command was 3,086. Then in case of unforeseen developments, Arnold notified the command at North Castle (as well as the one at South Salem) about a possible visit from a John Anderson.

But Arnold had come up with a new plan. Joshua Smith's house, he decided, would be an ideal meeting place. It was easily reached by water, either from Dobbs Ferry or from the British ship, *Vulture*. The only problem was that Joshua's family, Mrs. Smith and the two children, should not be there at the time. On the 14th when Benedict went to the Smiths' to meet Peggy and Edward, he explained to Joshua what he had in mind. He didn't mention John Anderson, only Beverly Robinson (who Arnold supposed would be coming too), and Joshua agreed to cooperate. He promised to take his wife and children to Fishkill to visit his sister Martha so the house would be empty on September 20.

Arnold had one more instruction. Joshua was to find a boat and oarsmen to take him to the *Vulture* to pick up Mr. Robinson who would be on board and perhaps another gentleman. They would spend the night at Joshua's and Arnold would come down the following day.

On September 15 and again on the 17th Arnold wrote André about the new plan. He said he would send a person to the *Vulture* on Wednesday, the 20th, between eleven and twelve o'clock at night to conduct him to a "place of safety." Indirectly he let André know that the person would be Joshua Smith.

Everyone seemed to be happy with the plans.

Clinton was relieved. Since André would be on board the *Vulture* going to a "a place of safety," he would have no need for a disguise. Trying to set aside his worries, Clinton went ahead with the next step. He was preparing his troops and transports to move up the Hudson as soon as André returned with the plans.

André was happy to be getting on with the act. He would have enjoyed the picture of himself rowing across the Hudson at midnight to a secret rendezvous. But this was just the first in a series of heroic scenes he had in mind. Clinton had promised that when the time came he would lead the attack on one of the principal forts at West Point.

As for Arnold, he was happy to think that it would soon be over. He had managed the plot well, he thought. On the morning of the 21st, he would tell his aides that he was going to inspect the garrison at Verplanck's Point. After he had done that, he would continue down to Smith's house and make final plans with André. He fully expected that within a few weeks the British would have won the war, he'd have his money, and he and Peggy would be starting a new life.

The only person who was not happy on September 20 was Joshua Hett Smith. He had his family safely out of the way, but he couldn't find a boat. When he inquired at King's Ferry for the boat he was supposed to have, he was told that there was none available. But then Joshua didn't have any oarsmen either, so he decided to arrange for them first. From the beginning, Joshua Smith must have counted on either or both of the Cahoon brothers for this job. They were his tenant farmers and would know better than to give away a secret. And who else could he count on? After all, it was risky to ask a man to row secretly at night to a British sloop of war. So Smith rode home, found Samuel Cahoon, took him inside his house, and told him about the errand.

Samuel Cahoon was an independent kind of man. He said he "had no mind" to row down the river.

Since Smith didn't have a boat anyway, he decided to drop the subject, but of course he had to let Arnold know how matters stood. So he asked Samuel to take a message to General Arnold. It was about a 30-mile ride, round trip.

Samuel said he had no mind to do that either. This time, however, Smith insisted and eventually Samuel agreed. He delivered the message at the Arnold residence at about sunrise.

Meanwhile André was on board the *Vulture*, waiting. He and Beverly Robinson had arrived at about seven in the evening and had watched the night darken from the deck of the sloop. The river here is about 2 miles wide and the *Vulture* was anchored on the east side near a point of land owned by a Mr. Teller. André, however, was not interested in the view of Mr. Teller's farm. He was straining to see the other shore, straining to hear some sound on the water. The hours crawled by. Midnight came and went. The early morning hours slipped past. But there was no boat. This was the second meeting that had failed to take place. What did it mean? André asked. Was the whole plot a trick? He couldn't return a third time without arousing suspicion among the British themselves. Indeed, there would be questions if even now he remained on board longer than his scheduled visit. Still, something might be worked out for the following night if he found an excuse to prolong his stay. So André pretended to be sick. He coughed and blew his nose. He was coming down with a cold, he said, and he had a terrible stomachache. When Beverly Robinson and Captain Sutherland urged that he stay an extra day until he felt better, André was quick to agree.

Of course they had to let Arnold know that André was still there. Captain Sutherland offered to send a message ashore, complaining that one of his smaller boats, proceeding under a white flag, had been fired on by the Americans. André wrote out the letter and below Sutherland's signature, he signed it: "John Anderson, Secretary." Beverly Robinson also wrote to Arnold, saying that he hoped Mr. Smith would come as soon as possible to conclude their business.

When Arnold received the message, he set about making plans for that night (September 21). He sent his own barge to find a boat and arranged to have it towed to a creek near Smith's house. Arnold himself arrived at the house about sunset. Now there was only the matter of the oarsmen.

Smith stopped Samuel Cahoon as he was on the way to bring in the cows. He was needed to row the boat tonight, Smith said.

Samuel said he had no mind to. He'd been up all night riding back and forth to General Arnold's and he was tired.

Smith told him to go into the house; General Arnold wished to speak with him. But Samuel Cahoon could say "No" to General Arnold as easily as anyone. He simply had no mind to go out in a boat at midnight, he said. Why couldn't it be done the next day?

It was a secret mission, Arnold explained, and very important.

Samuel said he was afraid the American guard boats might fire on him.

The boats would not fire, Arnold said. Mr. Smith knew the countersign for the night.

Well, Samuel said, he was afraid to go alone.

Joshua Smith told him to go and get his brother, Joseph.

When Samuel returned, Joseph was not with him. Instead, he had seen his wife and she would not *let* him go, he said.

Samuel was told again to get Joseph. But when the two of them came back, they were both firm. Neither one had a mind to go. At last General Arnold put an end to the argument. If they didn't go, he said, he'd put them under arrest. Toward midnight Smith gave the Cahoon brothers a quick drink to bolster their courage; Arnold promised them fifty pounds of flour as a reward. And with their oars muffled in sheepskin, Smith and the Cahoons set off for the 6-mile row down the black river and across to the *Vulture*.

It was a moonless night and although the Cahoons reached the *Vulture* safely, they were greeted by the British with what Smith later called "a volley of oaths." The sailors, who knew nothing of the errand, continued to exercise their vocabulary on the Cahoons while Smith went aboard to get his passenger. But to Smith's surprise, Beverly Robinson said he was sending a Mr. John Anderson in his place. It didn't matter to Smith, of course, who went with him, yet there was something strange about the change of plans. This Mr. Anderson, wrapped up in a long blue cloak, sat beside him in the stern of the boat and had little to say. But Smith took it for granted that he would be part of the conference and would find out the full story once they met with Arnold who was waiting in the woods up the riverbank.

But Smith was not to be part of any conference. Arnold dismissed him when he came, directing him to wait in the boat with the Cahoons while he and Anderson talked in the woods. The plan was that if the two men completed their business in time, Anderson would be returned to the *Vulture* that same night. If not, he would spend the day at Smith's house and be returned the following night. No one had consulted the Cahoons. And at four in the morning when Arnold told Smith that Mr. Anderson was ready to return, the Cahoons said there was no need to talk of it. They would not go. Neither Smith nor Arnold argued. Instead, mounting the two horses that Arnold had brought with him, Arnold and André set off for Joshua Smith's

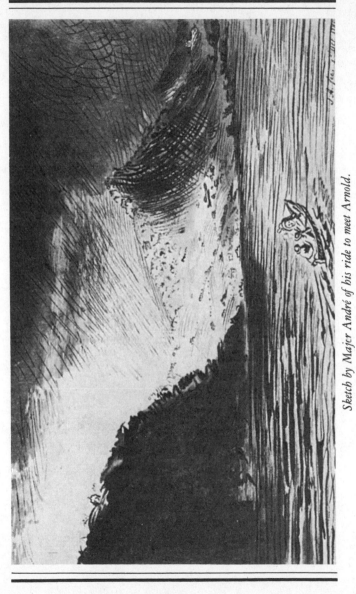

Sketch by Major André of his ride to meet Arnold.

house. (Joshua went with the Cahoons to moor the boat in the creek.)

Major André had no exact idea where Joshua Smith's house was. Certainly he did not know it was behind the American lines until he and Arnold were stopped by a sentry who gave the password of the night. Arnold answered with the countersign and although they passed on without incident, André felt that the situation was somehow slipping out of his control. This was not the script he had expected to follow.

Joshua Smith must have felt the same way. He had gone to great trouble for the General and had not thought he'd spend the night cramped in a boat with his two tenant farmers. Furthermore, when he served breakfast to General Arnold and Mr. Anderson, he had not expected Mr. Anderson to be sitting at the table in a British officer's uniform. Although General Arnold took him aside and explained that Mr. Anderson was a merchant who was wearing a borrowed British uniform because it pleased his vanity, Joshua Smith must have had second thoughts about his job.

Indeed, nothing seemed to be going according to the original plans. Colonel James Livingston, in command at Verplanck's Point, had become so irritated by the presence of the *Vulture* that, unknown to Arnold, he had managed to move two small cannons to Teller's Point. While Arnold and André were eating breakfast, Livingston opened fire, hitting the *Vulture* repeatedly and finally forcing it to move down the river. Watching the action from a window of the Smith house, Arnold and André realized that André might not be able to board the *Vulture* at all. They would have to make an alternate plan for getting André back to New York by land. Actually, there was only one way it could be done, Arnold said. Joshua Smith would have to accompany André to White Plains. And André would have to assume a disguise.

Benedict Arnold had no time, however, to decide these matters now. He had to get back to headquarters and would leave everything to Joshua Smith. The meeting had been a success, Arnold felt, and he was satisfied that he had left nothing undone. He and André had gone over the strategy for taking West Point. They had more or less settled the money matter. Clinton had offered to pay 6,000 pounds but André thought he could persuade him to raise it to 10,000, the amount that Arnold had originally proposed for his part in the plot, whether successful or not.

Now for the business at hand. Arnold wrote out passes which would take Smith and André past American guards. Then he took the plans he had made of West Point, enclosed them in six separate unsealed envelopes, and told André to take off his boots. The envelopes were to be placed between his stockings and his feet, Arnold said. Three in each boot.

And André did it. He knew, of course, that he was disobeying Clinton's orders. He must have known that there was nothing in writing that he would not remember or could not memorize. But he did not argue. Perhaps he was overwhelmed by how far events were taking him. Perhaps he was awed by the commanding personality of Benedict Arnold. Perhaps he thought Clinton should see the plans in Arnold's own handwriting. Or perhaps the risks simply seemed small to an inexperienced and bedazzled secret agent.

Still, he resisted Arnold's plan for travel by land. He did not want to wear a disguise. He did not wish to pass American guards. And indeed as the day wore on, there seemed no need to. The *Vulture* had only dropped down the river a few miles, just far enough to be out of firing range. There was no reason, André insisted, why he couldn't be returned to the sloop in his uniform as he had come.

But Joshua Smith had reasons of his own. The river would be dangerous tonight, he explained. After the morning bombardment, every guard boat would be out. And how would they get to the *Vulture*? Joshua didn't waste his breath trying to explain the Cahoons. Nor did he mention what was probably his primary reason. If he traveled by land, Joshua could turn off at some point and go directly to Fishkill for his wife and children. Then he could go home and take up his normal life. He'd be done with this Mr. Anderson.

At sunset Joshua Smith, allowing Mr. Anderson no choice in the matter, handed him a wine-colored jacket and a civilian's round beaver hat to replace his uniform. The jacket, although once a fancy one with gold lace buttonholes, was worn-looking with a tear in the sleeve; the beaver hat was scruffy. Yet much as he hated the shabby disguise, Major André did as he was told. Then he mounted the brown horse that Smith gave him and the two men set off: André a twenty-nine-year-old slightly built man, uneasy about the role he was being forced to play; and Joshua Smith, a plump, red-faced, hearty thirty-one-year-old with a loud greeting for everyone on the road.

André fully expected to travel most of the night to White Plains. The last part of the trip, he knew, would be through a sort of no-man's-land between American and British lines. This was a dangerous area fought over by roving bands from both parties. Tory bandits (or "Cowboys") had so devastated the countryside that many residents had just given up and moved out. The so-called Skinners were also on the road. They might be Patriots, trying to get even with the Cowboys and perhaps pick up some loot in the bargain, or they might simply be highwaymen, taking advantage of the general lawlessness to rob anyone they pleased. So if André seemed nervous and quiet at the beginning of such a journey, it was not surprising.

Indeed, the ride seemed to André to consist of a series of small crises. Apparently there was no way to restrain Joshua Smith from being sociable. At King's Ferry (where they crossed the river) Joshua stopped to chat with the usual group of loungers who hung about the ferry landing. He made a special point of conferring with Colonel Livingston, the man who had fired upon the *Vulture*. He even accepted a bowl of punch and drank, sitting on his horse. Later he talked to a group of New York militia and was so eager to please, he invented answers to questions that seemed awkward.

How far were they going? the militia captain wanted to know. Surely they didn't mean to travel to White Plains at night?

Oh no, Joshua replied. They would spend the night at Colonel Drake's. Just down the road.

But Colonel Drake was not at home, the Captain said.

Well, then, they'd just go on to Major Strang's.

Major Strang had moved away, the Captain reported. He asked to see their passes. After he had noted that everything was in order, he advised Joshua and his friend to turn back and spend the night at the Miller house. The Cowboys were out tonight, he said.

Joshua thanked the Captain and turned his horse around. André, of course, did the same. At the Miller house there was one room available with one bed in the room. The two men would have to share the bed, which in itself was an uninviting prospect as far as André was concerned, and André would be further inconvenienced. He would have to go to bed with his boots on. Knowing what was inside his boots, he had no choice.

It was an uncomfortable night, but the fact that morning finally did arrive seemed to cheer André. He was more talkative now as they traveled. Indeed, after they had successfully passed the last sentry post, he began to talk of poetry and books with as much enthusiasm as if he were sitting in his parlor. Perhaps this sudden show of confidence prompted Smith to leave André sooner than he had originally intended or perhaps he had always planned to turn back after crossing the American lines. But when the farmwoman who gave them breakfast reported that the Cowboys had driven off all but one of her cows the night before, Smith decided then and there that he had done all he could for Mr. Anderson. He gave him a map, some Continental bills, shook his hand, and went on his way—first to report to Arnold and then to Fishkill.

André may actually have been relieved to see Joshua go. He was more likely to meet British scouts now rather than Patriots (or so he'd been told), and he had only to tell the British who he really was and he'd be all right. On the other hand, if he met Patriots, he still had his pass. He had only 15 miles to go through this so-called neutral but devastated country and he put his horse at a steady trot. It was a drizzly day and on all sides lay signs of violence. Abandoned houses. Burned barns. Pastures grown high with weeds. Apples rotting on the ground. At one point André stopped to ask a twelve-year-old boy the way to Tarrytown. (The boy remembered that André's horse had one white forefoot and a white star on his forehead.) At another point he pulled up at a well and asked fourteen-year-old David Hammond and his twelve-year-old sister Sally for a drink of water. (David remembered that the mane of André's horse was full of burrs.)

At Mekeel's Corners (south of Pleasantville) the

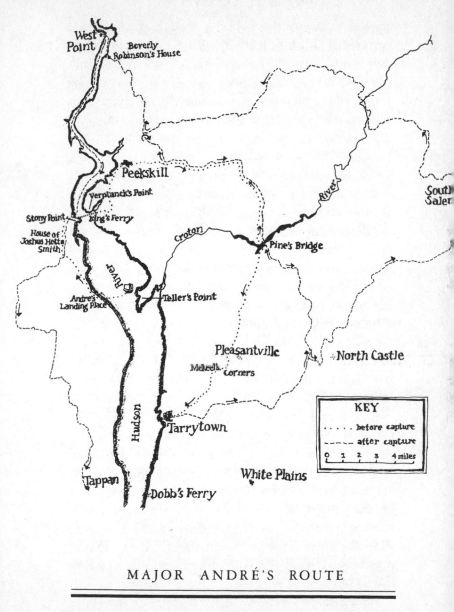

West Point

Beverly Robinson's House

Peekskill

Verplanck's Point

Stony Point

King's Ferry

House of Joshua Hett Smith

River

Croton

Pine's Bridge

River

South Salem

Andre's Landing Place

Teller's Point

Pleasantville

Meker's Corners

North Castle

Hudson

Tarrytown

Tappan

Dobb's Ferry

White Plains

KEY

. . . . . before capture

– – – – after capture

0 1 2 3 4 miles

MAJOR ANDRÉ'S ROUTE

road divided. André had the choice of taking the road through Tarrytown to White Plains or the one that went toward Dobbs Ferry. He chose the Tarrytown road. At nine-thirty in the morning he was reading his map as he approached the bridge leading into Tarrytown. Suddenly he was stopped.

For the last two hours three young men had been waiting for just such a stranger to come by. Members of the New York militia, they were on leave with permission to scout. All of them had family or friends who had suffered at the hands of Cowboys, so they were eager for revenge. All could use whatever booty they might pick up on a successful mission. Horses, money, watches, guns—everything was the legal property of Patriots who overtook the enemy. After arriving at the bridge, the three had drawn lots to see who would stand watch. Isaac Van Wort lost. While he stood near the road, the other two, David Williams (twenty-three and the oldest of the group) and John Paulding, sat in the bushes and played cards. John Paulding was the most conspicuous of the group. An extremely tall man, he was wearing a green jacket faced with red, part of the uniform worn by German mercenaries in the British army. Just four days before, a friend had smuggled this jacket into the British prison in New York where he was being held a captive. Wearing the jacket, he had been able to make his escape and he had worn it ever since.

When André stopped, he was impressed by John Paulding in his green jacket.

Paulding pointed his musket at André and asked where he was going.

Assuming from Paulding's jacket that he was with friends, André answered in a lighthearted way. "My lads," he said, "I hope you belong to our party."

"And what party is that?" Paulding asked.

André still had a chance to revise his lines but he must already have practiced what he would say and do if he met Tories, for he answered without hesitation. "Why, the lower party," he said. (This was a common way of referring to Tories, while "the upper party" referred to Patriots.) "I am a British officer," André volunteered, "and have been up the country on particular business and do not wish to be detained a minute." As proof, he took out his gold watch and showed it to the men. Few Americans owned gold watches and in the British army only those with a high rank would be likely to have one. (He also had a silver watch with him.)

John Paulding looked at the watch; then he informed André that he and his friends were American Patriots.

André tried valiantly to recover himself. He forced a laugh. "God bless my soul!" he said. "A body must do anything to get along nowadays." He took out Arnold's pass and handed it to Paulding.

The only one of the three who could read, Paulding looked it over, decided that it seemed valid, yet he was not satisfied.

"What is your name?" he asked.

"John Anderson."

It was the same name that appeared on the pass, yet Paulding was interested in a man with a gold watch. He asked André to dismount and step into the woods where he would be out of sight. He wished to search him.

As André took off his clothes, David Williams examined each piece: his coat, his hat, his jacket, his vest, his shirt, his breeches, his undergarments, but all he could find were the watches and eighty dollars in Continental bills. André stood before his captors with nothing on but his white-topped riding boots. Paulding told him to sit down and take off his boots. He did so. Still nothing. Paulding was about to tell him to get dressed when one of the men noticed that his socks sagged a little. He was told to take off his socks. And, of course, there were the six unsealed envelopes with the plans of West Point in them.

When Paulding looked at them, he recognized at once that this man must be a spy. At first André tried to convince them that he'd obtained the papers from a stranger at Pine's Bridge. It did not seem a likely story. So André offered the men money to let him go. His horse. His bridle. One hundred guineas (twenty-one shillings in gold). One thousand guineas even. He would stay while one of the men went to the British lines for the money. For a while his captors may have been tempted, but they sensed that here was something too big for them to handle. They decided to turn him over to the authorities at North Castle.

The three captors, joined by four friends, took turns leading André's horse (with André on it) while the others walked on each side to prevent his escape. They were full of questions but André would answer none of them. He had talked too much. He wasn't used to being a secret agent and he had done badly. He could hardly imagine a worse scene than the one he'd just been through in the woods, yet he knew there could be worse scenes ahead. He knew that only luck could help him now.

And indeed it seemed at North Castle that he might be lucky. Colonel Jameson, who was in command, remembered Arnold's orders: If John Anderson arrives, send him to West Point. Since this was John Anderson, there seemed nothing to do but follow orders. If it seemed strange that Anderson was traveling in the wrong direction and carrying dangerous-looking papers, he was sure that the General would straighten it all out. He did, however, take one precaution. Since he knew that General Washington was now en route from Hartford to Peekskill, he sent a messenger to intercept him and give him the dangerous-looking papers. But André would be at West Point before Washington could act, so André came close to safety.

André and his escort were only a half hour from Arnold's headquarters when his luck gave out. It happened after twenty-six-year-old Major Tall-madge, who had been away on a scouting expedition, returned to North Castle. And Major Tall-madge, in charge of Washington's secret service, was a more realistic man than Colonel Jameson. As soon as he heard the story, he guessed that General Arnold was committing treason and he persuaded Jameson to send someone after Anderson to get him back. But on one point Jameson would not yield. He insisted that he would send a messenger to Arnold with a letter explaining what had taken place. He did not consider that this letter might give Arnold a chance to escape if, in fact, Arnold was guilty.

Major André was stopped, brought back to North Castle, and then sent under an escort headed by Major Tallmadge to the post at South Salem. In his dirty and worn clothes, André did not give the impression of being anyone of importance, but from the first Major Tallmadge had noticed his walk. A soldier's walk with sharp, disciplined turns. And when the barber came the next morning to shave him, he noticed evidence of powder in his hair. This was a sure sign of a gentleman. Ordinary men did not wear powder in their hair.

As it turned out, André did not need to keep up his pretense for long. As soon as he learned that the West Point papers had been sent to Washington, he knew there was no point in keeping his identity a secret. What he had to do now was to convince the Americans that he was a prisoner of war and not a spy. It was an important distinction: prisoners of war were exchanged; spies were hanged.

On Sunday, September 24 (the day after his capture), he wrote General Washington, explaining who he was and describing his unfortunate position. He had not *meant* to go behind the American lines, he said, but had been taken against his will. He had not *meant* to venture through enemy territory. He had asked to be returned to the

Vulture but his wishes had been ignored. In effect, he had been made a prisoner and had been forced to wear a disguise. This did not account for the papers in his boots; nevertheless André was optimistic. He could not imagine that an adjutant general of the British army could ever be branded as a common spy.

On Thursday, September 28, André was transferred to Tappan, New York, where he was to be tried. Again Major Tallmadge, with whom André had become friendly in the last days, was in charge of the transfer. Finding a chance to talk privately, André asked Tallmadge what he thought would happen.

Benjamin Tallmadge had been a close friend and college classmate of Nathan Hale, the American officer who had gone on a secret mission disguised as a schoolteacher. The British had caught him behind their lines and hanged him as a spy. Tallmadge did not want to answer André's question, but when pressed, he reminded him of Nathan Hale.

"But surely you do not consider his case and mine alike?" André asked.

"Yes," Tallmadge replied. "Precisely the same."

BENEDICT ARNOLD HAD ALWAYS
hated to wait for action to begin and he hated it
now. Although he knew from Joshua Smith that all
had gone well with John Anderson, yet he would
have to wait to find out if André had really reached
New York safely. He would have to wait longer yet
for Clinton to start his movement up the Hudson.
Meanwhile Benedict Arnold would have to pretend
that he wasn't waiting for anything. He would have
to give the impression that he was actually
concerned with the defense of West Point. He
would have to extend his friendship to old friends as
if they would always be old friends. He would have
to hold in his restlessness and guard his tongue.
And this would be particularly hard on this
Monday morning, September 25. General Washington and his party were expected for breakfast.

Actually, three different parties were on their
way to Arnold's headquarters that morning.
Washington and his group (which included twenty-

three-year-old Alexander Hamilton, General Lafayette, General Knox and others) had come from Hartford by the upper road, not the lower road that Colonel James had believed they would be on. So the messenger carrying the dangerous-looking papers to Washington had returned to North Castle and had been sent out again on Sunday night with instructions to deliver the papers to Washington at Arnold's headquarters. A second messenger was also on the road. This one, having returned André to North Castle, was carrying Jameson's letter back to Arnold. Both messengers, traveling separately, spent the night on the way and continued Monday morning.

Washington's party was the first to arrive, but Washington decided to inspect some fortifications before going to the house. He asked his aides to tell Mrs. Arnold not to wait for him but to go ahead with breakfast. Mrs. Arnold, however, was not playing hostess this morning. Perhaps she didn't trust herself to appear as calm as she knew she must; in any case, she said she was ill, stayed in bed, and ate fresh peaches. Arnold, his own aides, and Washington's aides were at the breakfast table when one of the messengers from North Castle arrived. Luckily for Arnold, this was the messenger who had the letter that Jameson had written, telling him that John Anderson had been captured and papers found on him had been sent to General Washington.

Excusing himself from the table, Arnold ordered his horse to be brought to the door and his barge to be brought to the river landing. He ran up the steps, told Peggy the news, ran down the steps, and explained that he had been called on urgent business to West Point. Washington's party was just now approaching. Arnold asked his aides to make his apologies; he would be back in an hour, he said. Then he flung himself on his horse, plunged down the steep incline to the river, jumped on his black and gold barge, and ordered his oarsmen to hurry down the river. With his pistols cocked, he kept repeating that they must hurry, hurry. General Washington was expecting him, he said, and he must be back as soon as possible. When the barge approached the garrisons at Stony Point and at Verplanck's Point, Arnold tied a white handkerchief on the end of his cane and held it up as a flag of truce. The oarsmen, who had thought they were going to one of these garrisons, were told to continue. They were going to the *Vulture*, Arnold said, with a message to the Captain from General Washington. And as reward for their service, Arnold promised the oarsmen two gallons of rum.

It was 18 miles from Arnold's headquarters to the *Vulture,* but as soon as Arnold was on deck, he knew he was safe. Privately in the captain's quarters, he explained to Beverly Robinson and Captain Sutherland what had happened. Then stepping back on deck, he faced his eight oarsmen, who had also come on board. About to speak for the first time as a British officer, he used his conquering-hero voice that had inspired so many ordinary men to follow him into so many dangerous places. First, he explained why he had decided to support the British. Then as if he were offering his oarsmen a golden opportunity, he went on.

"If you will join me, my lads," he said, "I will make sergeants and corporals of you all." He turned to James Larvey, the coxswain. "And for you, James," he said, "I will do something more."

James had always been a favorite with Benedict and he thought James surely would not leave him. "No, sir," James replied. "One coat is enough for me to wear at a time."

Shamed before the British, Benedict promptly had all his oarsmen thrown into the hold as prisoners of war. (In New York General Clinton released them on parole.) Then Benedict wrote General Washington a letter which he left at Verplanck's Point for delivery. He used the self-righteous tone he would always use when he spoke of his treason, although he never used the word (surely not even to himself).

"The heart which is conscious of its own rectitude," he wrote, "cannot attempt to palliate a step which the world may censure as wrong. I have ever acted from a principle of love to my country . . . The same principle of love to my country actuated my present conduct, however it may appear inconsistent to the world, who very seldom judge right of any man's actions." Then he asked Washington to protect Peggy. "She is as good and as innocent as an angel," he wrote. "I beg she may be permitted to return to her friends in

Philadelphia, or to come to me, as she may choose."

By the time Washington had received the letter (at seven in the evening) he knew about the treason, had alerted the army, and was convinced of Peggy's innocence. Indeed, Peggy had put on a show that had won the sympathy of every officer at Arnold's headquarters and brought tears to the eyes of some. Naturally when she learned that the plot had failed, Peggy went into hysterics. Yet she timed her outburst carefully so that Arnold would have a chance to make his escape and Washington would not be in the house. Then she simply let herself go or she deliberately staged a "mad" scene that convinced everyone who saw it. Running into the hall, her hair and clothes in disarray, she began screaming that her child was going to be killed! Yes, he was! There was an order to kill him! When a doctor was called to give her a sedative, she protested that no one could help her but General Washington himself. She had a hot iron in her head, she cried, and only he could take it off. But when Washington later came back to the house (after failing to find Arnold at West Point), Peggy insisted that this man was not Washington. He was someone else who was going to kill her child. And where was General Arnold? He had irons in his head too, she shrieked, and he would never come back. Never! He was up there . . . there . . . there. She pointed wildly at the ceiling.

Everyone agreed that only an innocent woman could be shocked into such a frenzied state. So she was comforted, coddled, and pitied until at last she was able to compose herself. When Washington offered her a chance to go to New York or Philadelphia, she chose Philadelphia. Perhaps after her display of innocence, she could not easily choose to go to the man who (in the view of all present) had betrayed her as well as the country. Or perhaps since the plot had failed, she genuinely preferred to go back to the comfort and security of her childhood home. In any case, the Pennsylvania Council, unlike the American officers at West Point, was not impressed by her innocence. Once she was home, the Council set a deadline after which she would have to leave the state. "She was obliged, against her will," her brother-in-law wrote, "to go to the arms of a man who appears to be so very black." Yet since Peggy had chosen to play innocent, there is no way of knowing whether she truly went against her will or not.

At the moment, however, the country was less interested in Peggy Arnold or in Benedict Arnold than they were in Major André. Spy or not, he had caught the imagination of Americans. He was so young and so handsome and so talented, and after all, he had only been doing his duty. Indeed Americans became so emotionally involved in the fate of young Major André, it was as if he had suddenly become the brother, son, husband, or lover of each one. If only they could give André his freedom, they said, and get their hands on Arnold! Although such an exchange was suggested, there was no way the British could comply, no matter how much they might want to.

Major André was not unaware of the impression

he was making. He was in the center of the largest stage that he had ever occupied and although he surely would not have chosen his role, he knew how to play it. Familiar as he was with stories of heroes in history and literature, he understood exactly what was called for. Threatened with death, a hero was gallant. And when John André reached for gallantry, he found it. Stories of his unfailing courtesy, his cheerfulness, his fortitude spread through the country and as people listened, they sighed. Alexander Hamilton talked of André's "elegance of mind and manners." Major Tallmadge said André had "endeared himself" to him. And André himself, who could never resist noting his successes, wrote that he received "the greatest attention from His Excellency, General Washington."

The trial was held on Friday, September 29, with fourteen generals serving as judges. Although by this time André had received a fresh supply of clothes and a proper uniform from New York, he wore Joshua Smith's frayed jacket to the trial. When he spoke, he used the same arguments which he had first submitted in his letter to Washington and which seemed to him so simple and clear. After all, spies were generally "mean characters" who did their jobs for money, not men of rank and reputation. Major André called himself an "intermediary." Yet he must have prepared himself for the worst, for when the judges announced their unanimous decision that Major André was indeed a spy and "ought to suffer death," he did not lose his composure. He had determined to die a courageous death but he hoped he could at least choose the method. Back in his room, he wrote Washington, begging to be allowed the honor of a soldier's death. In other words, he wanted to be shot by a firing squad, not hanged like a criminal.

Everyone, Americans and British alike, mourned the verdict. General Clinton asked Washington for a reprieve; Benedict Arnold threatened revenge if the verdict was carried out; Alexander Hamilton begged Washington to let André die the way he wanted. Washington stood firm. Spies were hanged he said. If André were not hanged he could not be called a spy. The execution was set for Monday, October 2, at noon.

John André's good humor and courage never wavered. Those who were with him during his last days found it hard to match his spirits, yet André would not allow anyone to be downhearted. Raising his glass, he would ask for good cheer. Once when his servant broke down in front of him, André sent him out of the room. "Leave me," he said, "until you can show yourself more manly."

On the morning of his execution, André woke early, if indeed he had slept at all. To fill time, he did what he'd always enjoyed doing. He drew a pen and ink sketch of himself, sitting relaxed, sideways in a chair, his legs crossed, one arm extended on a table. The officer of the guard who was with him, twenty-year-old Jabez Tomlinson, noted that he used no mirror, yet the likeness was unmistakable. John André had made many self-portraits in the past and was well acquainted with his features. He looks composed in the drawing—on the verge, it seems, of smiling at some light remark made by a friend offstage. There are ruffles at his neck and wrists; he is an elegant young gentleman who betrays no hint that time will not go on for him in its careless, day-by-day way indefinitely. When he had finished the sketch, he gave it to Jabez.

André ate his breakfast (sent by General Washington from his own table), shaved, and dressed himself carefully in his uniform. Meanwhile outside his quarters five hundred American soldiers were assembling; in a field half a mile away hundreds (some say thousands) of spectators were gathering around a gallows. Among them were John Paulding, David Williams, and Isaac Van Wort. (They had been given André's horse, saddle, and watches and would soon be awarded a pension by Congress and 200 acres of land each.) The fourteen judges were lined up on horseback beside the road. Indeed, all officers at the army's Tappan headquarters were present with the exception of General Washington and his aides. Washington ordered all the blinds in his house (which overlooked the gallows) to be drawn, and out of respect for André whom he could neither save nor accommodate, he stayed inside.

At twelve o'clock the door of the tavern where André had been imprisoned opened. As the army's fife and drum corps struck up the Dead March, André, with his arms linked with an American officer on each side, half ran down the steps of the

Major André self-portrait on the morning of his execution.

tavern and through the double line of soldiers. At the sight of André, the crowd let out one agonizing cry and then fell silent, watching as he raised his hat and bowed to the row of generals who had been his judges. He faltered only when he saw the gallows and then just briefly. "It will soon be over," he murmured as he proceeded to the wagon which was drawn up under a dangling noose. For a moment André stood beside the wagon, looking down at the ground, rolling a small stone over and over with his foot. Then, as if that were the last unrehearsed bit of action he would allow himself, he pulled himself up on the wagon.

The commanding officer in charge of the execution read the order and then addressed the prisoner. "Major André," he said, "if you have anything to say, you can speak, for you have but a short time to live."

His hands on his hips, André bowed to the officer and spoke his final lines so clearly, they were heard by the entire audience.

"I have nothing more to say, gentlemen, than this: I pray you to bear witness that I meet my fate like a brave man."

André handed his hat to his servant, unbuttoned his shirt collar, turned it down, and refusing the services of the hangman, he put the noose around his own neck. He took two silk handkerchiefs from his pocket. With one, he blindfolded himself. The other, he gave to the hangman to tie his arms.

The commanding officer ordered the wagon to be pulled out from under André's feet. The last sound that André heard was probably the crack of the wagoner's whip as the horses leaped forward with the wagon.

The army doctor in attendance reported that the spectators seemed to be overwhelmed by the event. "There did not appear to be one hardened or indifferent spectator," he said, "in all the multitude."

As the country mourned for André, it became more and more enraged at Arnold. In Philadelphia, in Boston, in Providence, in towns all over Connecticut, crude images (or effigies) of Arnold were made, carried through the streets, and burned. Often Arnold was shown with the devil beside him or leaning over his shoulder. Yet beneath all the anger people kept asking the same question over and over.

How could he have done it?

One person who would not have been surprised at Benedict Arnold's treason was John Brown. Three years before he had all but predicted it. "Money is this man's god," he had written "and to get enough of it he would sacrifice his country." At the time of the treason John Brown was in Mohawk County, fighting Indians. He was killed before he could hear the news.

chapter
· 12 ·

WHEN AN AIDE REMARKED TO Washington that Benedict must be going through the torments of hell as he reflected on what he had done, Washington shook his head. "No," he said. "He wants feeling."

Yet Benedict was certainly shaken by the news that André had actually been hanged and, of course, Peggy, who still had that lock of André's hair, was shaken too. Nevertheless, within a few days of the hanging, Arnold was haggling over the price of his services, asking for the 10,000 pounds that André had thought Clinton might pay. Although Clinton was still in shock over the death of a young man he had loved as a son, Arnold wrote him. "I believe you will not think my claim unreasonable," he wrote, "when you consider the sacrifices I have made." Apparently Clinton did think that the claim was unreasonable, for Arnold was paid just 6,000 pounds plus expenses.

Benedict Arnold never seemed to grasp the

enormity of what he'd done. Sometimes he acted as if his treason were nothing more than a switch in political parties. He actually took the trouble to write a formal letter of resignation from the Continental army as if he had not already automatically cut all his ties with America. He even wrote Congress demanding his back pay. When he published an explanation of his actions "To the Inhabitants of America," he made his treason sound like a simple change of mind. When he "quitted domestic happiness for the perils of the field," he wrote, he had wanted only to settle disagreements with Britain, not to separate from it. There had been, of course, many times when Arnold had declared himself publicly for independence, but he overlooked all evidence (even his oath of loyalty) that was not convenient. Benedict Arnold always had, and always would, believe just what he wanted to believe.

And, of course, in spite of the failure of his conspiracy, he wanted to believe that he was a hero. He had wanted Clinton to go ahead with his attack on West Point and had volunteered to lead it, but Clinton gave up that idea. There were other ways that Benedict could still win the war for Britain, but the person he had to convince, he decided, was the man in London who was in charge of the war— Lord Germain, secretary of state for the colonies. So he wrote directly to Germain, telling him just what to do. First, he should promote Arnold to a major general. (Clinton had made him a brigadier general.) "I beg leave to observe . . . that the sacrifices of fortune I have made are great," he pointed out. With this recommendation out of the way, he went on with others. Offer to make General Washington a baron, he said, and he'd surely give up the idea of independence. Promise American soldiers back pay, pensions, and land. Allow troops of American Tories to participate in action. Two or three such divisions, he claimed, could force the American army to quit. "Believe me, my lord," he wrote, "this is not a visionary scheme, but what I know to be practicable."

Meanwhile Benedict Arnold set about to raise a corps of his own from among those presently serving in the Continental army. One thousand men, he hoped to get. He printed a proclamation, inviting all who had "the real interest of their country at heart" to join him in the British service. A lengthy proclamation, it was issued twice a week from October 25 through December 6. At the end of that time, a total of sixty men had volunteered: twenty-eight officers and thirty-two soldiers, including one drummer. This was not reassuring either to Arnold or to the British who had thought that the Continental army would fall now like a line of dominoes. Beginning with Arnold, each one would push over another. "When a ship is sinking," some cynical Tories had observed, "the rats leave." But contrary to expectation, Benedict Arnold's treason had strengthened, not weakened, the American will. Struggling to work together, many Americans had out of habit thought of themselves first as citizens of their separate colonies, but now that their whole country had been so brazenly betrayed, they drew together with a new sense of themselves as Americans.

Benedict and Peggy had been in New York two months now, living next door to General Clinton, participating in the social life of the city, but Benedict had not achieved the prominence he'd expected. British politics, he was beginning to discover, was no more farsighted than American; the British army was no more capable; and British generals were no more enterprising. Indeed, General Clinton was as much of a "Granny" as General Gates, and Arnold dreamed of the day when he might replace him in command. Meanwhile he had to prove himself. In order to attract more recruits, he had to prove himself. In order to impress Lord Germain, he had to prove himself. Benedict Arnold would never be done proving himself.

In December 1780, Clinton gave him his first chance. In command of an expedition of fifteen hundred men and supported by seven warships, Arnold was sent to Virginia to raid and destroy enemy property. Successful at every turn, he took Richmond, destroyed warehouses of public stores, and overcame resistance wherever he met it. He was untiring in his efforts, yet he could never throw himself into action in his old devil-may-care style. Knowing how desperately he was wanted by Americans, he no longer performed his solo acts of bravery in front of his troops. General Washington had made no secret of his wishes: he wanted Arnold taken alive and everyone knew why. Americans wanted to hang Benedict Arnold. Thomas Jefferson, however, was less particular. He offered 5,000 guineas to the person who would take him any way at all. Riflemen of the Virginia militia made a model of Arnold's head and used it for target practice. So at the end of his mission in Virginia, impressive as it was, Arnold's troops had no stories to tell of his personal heroism. Instead they talked of his lust for prize money. "His love of money, his ruling passion," it was reported, "has been very conspicuous in Virginia."

In June of 1781 Arnold was back in New York, restless as ever, critical of everyone, eager to take charge, threatening to quit. "General Arnold is discouraged," a prominent Tory wrote. "He can get nothing done."

He asked to attack West Point, but Clinton said, No. Philadelphia? No, again. Then he suggested a raid on the privateering port of New London, only 12 miles from his native Norwich, and Clinton agreed. Perhaps this would divert the French from the British general, Lord Cornwallis, who was having trouble in Yorktown, Virginia. On September 5 Arnold put his troops ashore on both sides of the river at New London while he went to a hillside behind the city to watch the action that he longed to lead. Again the mission was successful, although the death toll of the British was high. The expedition is remembered, however, for the atrocities that the British committed and for the fire they set. Although Arnold ordered that only warehouses and shops be set on fire, the wind carried the fire through the town, destroying two hundred homes. From his vantage point, Arnold would have watched a fire far bigger than any he'd set as a boy on Thanksgiving Eve, but there was no glory in it. Even the British deplored the destruction, although they didn't blame Arnold. Only the Americans did that. Those in his home state called him every evil name they knew and wished they could think of more.

The raid did nothing to help General Cornwallis. On October 19, surrounded on all sides by French and Americans, Cornwallis surrendered his entire army. It was such a massive victory for America that there were rumors the war might be over, but Benedict Arnold would listen to no such talk. The war could not be over; Britain could not have lost. He could not have chosen the wrong side. He would go immediately to England, tell them how to win, beg for reinforcements, and ask to be given Clinton's command. He would talk to the king.

On December 15, 1781, Benedict and Peggy sailed for London—Benedict in a warship in case Americans tried to capture him at sea, Peggy in a merchant ship. And in London Benedict did see the king. As it happened, Benedict and the king were in perfect agreement. Of course the war couldn't be over, King George said. He would not *allow* it to be over. The queen took a fancy to Peggy and the Arnolds were often seen at the palace.

Then there was an election in England. The Tory government that had been running the war was voted out and the new government was in favor of peace. Lord Germain no longer had a job and even the king could not have his way. The war was really over and Benedict Arnold was retired on an officer's half-pay. Peggy and the children would eventually receive pensions. (There would be a total of eight children: three from Benedict's first marriage; five from his marriage to Peggy.) Benedict Arnold made more money out of the war than any other American general, but he was never satisfied. Major André's brother, whose distinction was only that he *was* a brother, was made a baron. Benedict Arnold could never understand why a person with pure motives (and he never questioned his motives) would not be suitably honored. It was as if his whole life had been put on a scale and nothing counted but that one act at West Point which had failed by accident only. So why should so many British hold that against him?

"I care little what the herd of mankind say or think of me," he once said. Yet he did care. He simply had never learned that there was more required in life than grabbing on to mill wheels. He still believed that the way to be admired was to put on a show: exhibit courage and display wealth. And now that the war was over, he set about, as he had so often, to acquire wealth.

By 1785 he had his own brig and had established himself as a merchant-trader in St. John, New Brunswick (Canada), where so many American Tories had settled. Just as he had in his New Haven days, he traveled back and forth to the West Indies and he built a grand house on the waterfront of St. John for his family (in which he included Hannah and his three sons by his first marriage). Presumably he thought that a community of transplanted American Tories would prove congenial to live with, but it did not work out that way. Perhaps he set too much store by his fancy lifestyle, for he was proud of his mahogany beds, his blue damask curtains and his parlor furniture upholstered in blue damask, his Wedgewood giltware, his two sets of Nankeen china. His neighbors said he was haughty and cared more for money than for friendship. Yet when the citizens of St. John finally expressed their contempt, they condemned his present behavior less than his past behavior. They could not forgive his treason. They made an effigy of him, labeled it "Traitor," and burned it before his own front door. In effect, they were asking: Did he really think he'd be accepted as a Tory when he'd been *paid* to become one? A captain, who had been with Arnold in Quebec and was now working for him, remarked: "When I thought of what he had been and the despised man he then was, tears would come, and I could not help it."

Benedict Arnold must have longed to defend himself physically against that word "Traitor," to hurl himself against the name-callers, to get even, to prove his honor. He moved away from St. John in 1792, but back in London he had the same trouble.

One time, however, he did fight back. The Earl of Lauderdale, speaking openly in Parliament, called Benedict Arnold "the epitome of treason," and Benedict challenged him to a duel. Although the earl was not eager to fight, he was not willing to say (as Benedict insisted) that he had not meant to malign Arnold's character. He would only admit that he was sorry to have hurt his feelings, but this was not enough for Benedict. So on July 1, 1792, at seven o'clock in the morning the two men met with their seconds and their pistols. When it was time to shoot, Benedict misfired and the earl refused to fire at all. The earl decided then that rather than go through this a second time, he'd just say what Benedict wanted him to say. So he did and Benedict went home, satisfied. He was fifty-one years old now and was proud that at least on that day he had proved himself. Peggy wrote: "It has been highly gratifying to find the General's conduct so much applauded . . . particularly by a number of the first characters in the kingdom."

Peggy was not always so pleased, however, with her general who did not provide her with the income she thought she needed. She was sick of struggling, she complained, but for the sake of her children's future, it was necessary "to keep up appearances." This meant that she must have a carriage, a coachman, a home and clothes appropriate to her class and position. Those "appearances," she wrote her father, were "absolutely necessary in this Country to bring forward a young family." But Peggy knew how to manage money, how to scheme for patronage, and somehow she produced the necessary "appearances" in spite of her constant anxiety about the risks Benedict took and the debts he incurred.

What Benedict needed was a scene of action. As always when human relations became complicated, when he felt belittled in any way, he longed for an arena where there would be danger, conflict, challenge. In 1793 when England went to war against France, he thought he would have another chance. He planned just how he would destroy the French fleet but when he offered his services, he was turned down. So he went anyway in a private capacity. The West Indies, he knew, would be filled with French ships protecting French islands and British ships protecting British islands, and both trying to take each other's islands. He would find some way to participate in the danger and in the meantime he would trade, the profitable kind of trading that generally resulted from daring dangerous waters in wartime.

Once in the West Indies, he assumed the role of a secret agent, finding out French positions, estimating their strength, and then passing on the information to the British. He must have been helpful, for when he left, plantation owners on the British islands gave him a vote of thanks and the king gave him an acreage of land in upper Canada. In addition, Benedict made profits. Posing as an American trader, he slipped past French guns into a harbor, made his deals, and slipped away again. The profits he made on one island, however, he would lose on the next, but there were always more islands and who knew on which his fortune might lie?

An ordinary man might, however, have given up his dreams when he was captured by the French, but whatever was said about Benedict Arnold, no one ever accused him of being an ordinary man. He was taken aboard a French ship and asked who he was.

"An American trader," he replied.

"Your name?"

"John Anderson."

Perhaps the French captain was suspicious; in any case, he locked him up in a cabin. Later Benedict learned that the captain had discovered who he truly was and planned to hang him. For Benedict this was a moment for a mill wheel and he was not too old to accept the challenge. Secretly he pried up enough floor boards in the cabin so he could piece together a makeshift raft. That night he lowered it out the window and followed on a rope. Lying flat on his stomach and paddling the raft with his hands, he made his way through shark-infested waters to a rowboat moored nearby. He climbed into the boat, muffled the oars, and dodging among French ships, he finally found a British ship and was pulled to safety. As it turned out, this was the headquarters ship of General Charles ("No Flint") Grey, once Major André's commanding officer.

But as the war went on, Benedict Arnold began to fail physically and he became anxious. If there was one thing he did not want, it was to die helplessly in bed. He wanted a soldier's death, noble and quick. For two years (1797–99) he asked again and again for a command but was refused each time. Then in 1801, when he was sixty years old, he made a last desperate attempt at that quick fortune that had always eluded him. He took what savings he had, invested it in a privateer, and because of his weakened physical condition, he hired a captain. Nothing went right on this expedition. If Benedict had secretly hoped for a confrontation that might afford him a dignified death, he didn't even get that. Nor a fortune. Instead he came home with so many bills, the Arnolds were forced to sell the lease on their home and move to a smaller house.

Benedict Arnold suffered from asthma, gout, and dropsy, and, as Peggy said, his spirits were so broken and his nerves so destroyed "that he has been for a long time past incapable of the smallest enjoyment." Contrary to what George Washington believed, Arnold was a man who had always been beset by torments, not torments of guilt but torments just the same.

He died in bed on Sunday morning, June 14, 1801.

The report of his death was, of course, printed in American newspapers. Indeed it was the only way Americans would permit his name to appear— briefly on paper, never in permanent form. Citizens of Norwich had long ago torn up the headstones from the graves of Benedict Arnold's father, who was also named Benedict, and of his older brother who had died as an infant, another Benedict.

Even with the passing of time the scales are inevitably weighted down with his treason. Even a recent monument on the spot on the Saratoga battlefield where Benedict Arnold was wounded bears no name, only the carving of a military boot and a major general's epaulet. "In memory of the most brilliant soldier in the Continental Army," the inscription reads, "who was desperately wounded on this spot . . . 7th October, 1777, winning for his countrymen the decisive battle of the American Revolution."

In a small chapel at the United States Military Academy at West Point where plaques are dedicated to the memory of generals of the American Revolution, there is such a plaque for General Arnold, but his name does not appear. Only his dates:

1741–1801

notes

Page 9. Benedict Arnold has been variously described—from 5'6" to 5'9". Generally he was referred to as a man of "medium" height, although a member of second wife Peggy Shippen's family called him "Peggy's little general."

Page 16. It was not the king alone who had different ideas about governing the colonies. The governing party in Britain also supported a tax program. King George was influential but he did not have the power to make policy by himself.

Page 28. It is interesting to note that Benedict Arnold's official Massachusetts orders were signed by Benjamin Church, a member of the inner circle of Massachusetts revolutionaries, who turned out to be America's first traitor. He was in the pay of the British general in command of Boston.

Page 33. A local twelve-year-old boy served as a guide on the night that Fort Ticonderoga was captured.

Page 35. For lack of transportation, the cannons at Fort Ticonderoga were not moved until the following winter when they were dragged across the snow to Boston.

Page 49. Ethan Allen was kept for a month on a prison ship with 30-pound irons shackled to his legs. He was then sent to London, returned to Halifax, then to New York in October 1776. He was exchanged as a prisoner of war in the winter of 1778 and he returned to his home. He spent the rest of the war trying to get the Continental Congress to recognize Vermont as an independent state but he was unsuccessful. For a time he even secretly explored the possibility of having Vermont annexed to Canada.

Page 63. A gondola in eighteenth-century America referred to a large flat-bottomed gunboat.

Page 66. Benedict Arnold bought the dozen pair of silk hose from Paul Revere.

Page 67. John Adams was also exasperated at the conflicts among the representatives of the Continental Congress itself—at the timidity of some men; the self-interest, the hypocrisy of others.

Page 80. Americans referred to the three British generals—Howe, Clinton, Burgoyne—as "the three bow-wows."

Page 101. As a prisoner of war, André was put up in a Quaker home in Lancaster, Pennsylvania, where he became interested in teaching the twelve-year-old son in the house how to draw. Later André was transferred to Carlisle, Pennsylvania.

Page 109. Arnold did not, however, limit himself to the company of Tory ladies. Benjamin Franklin received a letter from his daughter, Sally, in which she told of a visit with Benedict Arnold. Sally had taken her little girl, Betty, with her. According to Sally, Betty gave "such old-fashioned smacks General Arnold says he would give a good deal to have her for a school Mistress to teach the young Ladies to kiss."

Page 141. Joshua Smith also sent his servants away during André's stay, so he had to serve the breakfast himself. He did retain one young slave who accompanied him on his ride with André. It didn't matter what the slave saw or heard since a slave's word could not be used in court or in any legal proceedings.

Page 148. Beside the bridge there was a giant tulip tree. The legend is that on the day the news arrived in Tarrytown that Arnold had died in England, the tulip tree was struck by lightning.

Page 153. Joshua Hett Smith, routed out of bed in Fishkill, was accused of being in on the treason. After a four-week-long trial, he was acquitted, but by order of Washington, he was held in jail in New York on further suspicions. He escaped in a woman's clothes. After the war, he moved to England and became a country gentleman.

Page 156. Needless to say, the oarsmen didn't get their rum, any more than the Cahoons got their flour.

Page 158. Benedict's sister, Hannah, was exceedingly distressed by news of the treason. "Let me ask the pity of all my friends," she wrote. "Forsake me not in my distress." Yet she did not forsake Benedict.

Page 159. On her return to Philadelphia, Peggy Arnold stayed overnight in Paramus, New Jersey, with Theodora Prevost, widow of a British officer. (She had also stayed with her on the way to West Point.) Theodora later married Aaron Burr, who reported (after both Arnolds were dead) that Peggy had confided in Theodora. She had said that she was sick of playacting and pretending she was innocent. There is no way of knowing if this is true or not, although it seems strange that Peggy, who was never known to confide in anyone about the treason, should have talked so freely with a relative stranger. Burr, however, was well known to the Shippens. Orphaned as a boy, he had stayed for a year in the care of the Shippen family in Philadelphia.

Aaron Burr (at one time vice-president of the United States) is best remembered for his fatal shooting of Alexander Hamilton in a duel. It is interesting to note that Burr was once tried on a charge of treason and although he was acquitted, popular opinion was strongly against him.

Page 165. The hangman was a Tory named Strickland who was under arrest but had been promised his freedom in return for this job. He had rubbed shoe-blacking over his face and hands so he wouldn't be recognized.

Page 173. A monument was raised to the memory of John André in Westminster Abbey, London. (The Arnolds were seen visiting it on one occasion.) In 1821 André's body was moved from Tappan to Westminster Abbey.

Page 174. Although Benedict Arnold was never popular in England, he did have friends. One of his closest friends was Lord Cornwallis.

Page 178. After Benedict Arnold's death, Peggy wrote home to her brother-in-law: "I have to deplore being left in very embarrassed circumstances . . . the last unfortunate speculation . . . of fitting out a privateer, has involved us in many difficulties . . . My sufferings are not of the present moment only,—years of unhappiness have past . . . you . . . are ignorant of the many causes of uneasiness I have had."

Yet she wrote Richard and Henry: "Your father's *motives,*

not the unfortunate termination of them, will make his memory doubly dear."

She did manage to pay off the accumulated debts and wrote: "I have not even a tea-spoon, a towel, or a bottle of wine that I have not paid for."

She was not well in her last years, often complaining about a "confusion in my head." "I cannot connect things or make arrangements," she said in the fall of 1801. Peggy died of cancer three years after Benedict's death.

bibliography

*(Sources that relate directly
to the characters)*

MANUSCRIPT SOURCES

Biddle Collection. (Letters of Benedict and Peggy Arnold.) Pennsylvania Historical Society. Philadelphia, Pennsylvania.

Schuyler Papers. New York Public Library. New York, N.Y.

PRINTED SOURCES

Abbatt, William. *The Crisis of the Revolution.* New York: William Abbatt, 1899.

Arnold, Isaac N. *The Life of Benedict Arnold.* Chicago: A. C. McClurg, 1880.

Bakeless, John. *Turncoats, Traitors, and Heroes.* New York: J. B. Lippincott, 1959.

Billias, George Athan, ed. *George Washington's Generals.* New York: William Morrow & Co., 1969.

———. *George Washington's Opponents.* New York: William Morrow & Co., 1969.

Boylan, Brian Richard. *Benedict Arnold: The Dark Eagle.* New York: W. W. Norton, 1973.

Butterfield, L. H., ed. *Adams Family Correspondence.* Vol. 2. New York: Atheneum, 1965.

Canning, Jeff, and Buxton, Wally. *History of the Tarrytowns.* Harrison, New York: Harbor Hill Books, 1975.

Caulkins, F. M. *History of Norwich, Connecticut.* Hartford: 1845.

Codman, John. *Arnold's Expedition to Quebec.* New York: Macmillan Co., 1903.

Connecticut Historical Society. *Collections.*

Continental Congress. *Journals.* Vol. VI, 1776 (Library of Congress, ed. 1904–1957).

Davis, Matthew. *Memoirs of Aaron Burr.* New York: Harper, 1855.

Decker, Malcolm. *Benedict Arnold, Son of the Havens.* 1932.
———. *Ten Days of Infamy.* New York: Arno Press, 1969.

Dexter, F. B. *Biographical Sketches of Yale Graduates.* Vol. III. 1903.

Dorson, Richard M., ed. *America Rebels.* New York: Pantheon, 1953.

Flexner, James Thomas. *The Traitor and the Spy.* Boston: Little, Brown, 1953.

Force, Peter, ed. *American Archives.* 4th and 5th Series. 6 vols. and 3 vols. Washington: 1837–46; 1848–53.

French, Allen. *The Taking of Ticonderoga in 1775.* Cambridge, Mass: Harvard University Press, 1928.

Fritz, Jean. *Cast for a Revolution.* Boston: Houghton Mifflin, 1972.

Hamilton, Edward P. *Fort Ticonderoga: Key to a Continent.* Boston: Little, Brown, 1964.

Hargreaves, Reginald. "Burgoyne and America's Destiny," *American Heritage,* Vol. 7, June 1956.

Howe, Archibald. "Colonel John Brown of Pittsfield, Massachusetts, An Address by Archibald M. Howe at the Village of Palatine Bridge, N.Y." Boston: W. B. Clarke Co., 1908.

Hudleston, F. J. *Gentleman Johnny Burgoyne.* Indianapolis: Bobbs-Merrill, 1927.

Hufeland, Otto. *Westchester County During the American Revolution.* Westchester County Historical Society, White Plains: 1926.

Jellison, Charles A. *Ethan Allen: Frontier Rebel.* Syracuse, New York: Syracuse University Press, 1969.

Lengyel, Cornel. *I, Benedict Arnold: The Anatomy of Treason.* New York: Doubleday, 1960.

Luzader, John. *Decision on the Hudson.* National Park Service: Department of the Interior, 1975.

Massachusetts Historical Society. *Proceedings.*

Moore, Frank. *Diary of the American Revolution.* New York: Charles T. Evans, 1863.

Morpurgo, J. E. *Treason at West Point: The Arnold-André Conspiracy.* New York: Mason/Charter, 1975.

Nickerson, Hoffman. *The Turning Point of the Revolution.* Boston: Houghton Mifflin, 1928.

Paine, Lauren, *Benedict Arnold: Hero and Traitor.* London: Robert Hale, 1965.

Palmer, Dave Richard. *The River and the Rock.* New York: Greenwood Publishing Company, 1967.

Pennsylvania Magazine of History and Biography. *Life of Margaret Shippen, Wife of Benedict Arnold.* Nos. XXI and XXV, 1900 and 1901.

Roberts, Kenneth, ed. *March to Quebec: Journal of the Members of Arnold's Expedition.* New York: Doubleday & Doran, 1938.

Sargent, Winthrop. *Life and Career of Major John André.* New York: Garrett Press, 1969.

Scharf, J. T. *History of Westchester.* Vol. II. Philadelphia: L. S. Preston, 1886.

Scheer, George, and Rankin, Hugh F. *Rebels and Redcoats.* New York: New American Library, 1959.

Sellers, Charles Coleman. *Benedict Arnold, the Proud Warrior.* New York: Minton, Balch, & Co., 1930.

Smith, J. E. A. *History of Pittsfield, Massachusetts.* 2 vols., Boston: 1869.

Smith, Joshua Hett. *Authentic Narrative of the Causes That Led to the Death of Major André.* London: 1808.

Sparks, Jared. *The Life and Treason of Benedict Arnold.* New York: Harper, 1856.

Thacher, James. *A Military Journal During the American Revolution.* Boston: Cottons & Barnard, 1827.

Todd, Charles Burr. *The Real Benedict Arnold.* New York: A. S. Barnes, 1903.

Van Doren, Carl. *The Secret History of the American Revolution.* New York: Viking, 1941.

Wallace, Willard M. *Traitorous Hero: The Life and Fortunes of Benedict Arnold.* New York: Harper & Row, 1954.

Ward, Christopher. *The War of the American Revolution.* New York: Macmillan, 1952.

Winsor, Justin. *Narrative and Critical History of America.* Vol. VI. Boston: Houghton Mifflin, 1888.

index